TREASURES OF THE
Musée d'Orsay

TREASURES OF THE
Musée d'Orsay

INTRODUCTION BY

Françoise Cachin

CHAPTER INTRODUCTIONS BY

Xavier Carrère

*Louve before 1820
Orsay 1820-1870
Beaubourg after 1870*

ARTABRAS

A DIVISION OF ABBEVILLE PUBLISHING GROUP

New York   London   Paris

Front cover: Detail of Edouard Manet, *Olympia,* 1863. See page 53.
Back cover: Vincent van Gogh (1853–1890). *The Artist's Bedroom in Arles,* 1889. Oil on canvas,
    22⅜ x 29⅛ in. (57 x 74 cm).
Frontispiece: Detail of Gustave Courbet, *The Painter's Studio: Allegory of Seven Years of
    My Artistic and Moral Life,* 1854–55. See page 30.
Page 6: Interior of the Musée d'Orsay.
Page 10: Exterior of the Musée d'Orsay.

Editor: Nancy Grubb
Translator: Carol Volk
Designer: Virginia Pope
Production Editor: Abigail Asher
Production Manager: Lou Bilka

All photographs are by Hubert Josse, except for those on pages 155, 184, 186–92, and 196–203, which are from the Réunion des Musées Nationaux, Paris.

First edition
10 9 8 7 6 5 4

Library of Congress Cataloging-in-Publication Data
Treasures of the Musée d'Orsay / introduction by Françoise Cachin ;
    chapter introductions by Xavier Carrère.
        p.   cm.
        Rev. ed. of: Treasures of the Musée d'Orsay, Paris.
        Includes index.
        ISBN 0-89660-054-8
        1. Art, Modern—19th century—Catalogs. 2. Art, Modern—20th century—Catalogs.
3. Art—France—Paris—Catalogs. 4. Musée d'Orsay—Catalogs. I. Cachin, Françoise.
II. Carrère, Xavier. III. Musée d'Orsay. IV. Title: Treasures of the Musée d'Orsay, Paris.
N6447.T69   1995
709'03'407444361—dc20   94-39367

CONTENTS

INTRODUCTION

Françoise Cachin

The end of the twentieth century has seen a growing interest in the intellectual and artistic creation of the previous century in Europe, before the fragmentation provoked by World War I. This current curiosity, possibly tinged with a bit of nostalgia, is embodied in the crowds of French and foreign visitors to the Musée d'Orsay: some thirty million to date, if we include those who have come to view the temporary exhibitions organized by the museum at the nearby Grand Palais. The connection between these two great structures, which were both conceived for the Exposition Universelle of 1900, is thus still alive and well one century later: the Grand Palais was and still is devoted to exhibitions; the Orsay train station and hotel, formerly intended to receive and house visitors arriving from southwestern Europe to the heart of Paris, has become the Musée d'Orsay.

"The train station is magnificent and looks like a palace of fine arts, and since the Palace of Fine Arts looks like a train station, I suggested to Laloux [the Orsay architect] that he switch them if there was still time!" wrote the academic painter Edouard Detaille in 1900, before the inauguration of the two buildings. His mission for the train station, at least, was accomplished as of December 1986.

Let's back up a bit to the circumstances that led to the preposterous concept of transforming a train station into a museum. This idea resulted from several changes that had occurred in the 1970s. In 1977 the transfer of the twentieth-century art collections to the Centre d'Art et de Culture Georges Pompidou (popularly known as the Beaubourg) left an entire segment of art, from Impressionism to Cubism, at the Palais de Tokyo (former site of the Musée National d'Art Moderne). The lack of space at the Jeu de Paume, the Impressionist museum, meant that masterpieces were being kept in storage, as was an entire group of paintings and sculptures at the Musée du Louvre that did not fit into any chronological or aesthetic category at either the Louvre or the Beaubourg. Meanwhile, there was a critical reevaluation taking place of nineteenth-century art that did not fit into the somewhat sectarian history of the avant-gardes; this complemented the desire to show the work of the period as a whole—its photography, architecture, furnishings, and objets d'art as well as its painting and sculpture. All of these forces made the creation of a new museum an urgent matter—a museum that would form a bridge between the Louvre and the Beaubourg.

Meanwhile, in the heart of Paris, a vacant building was in danger of being destroyed to make way for a hotel: the Orsay train station and hotel, opposite the Louvre and the Tuileries gardens. The building, which had been considered ugly only a few decades earlier—so distinctly was its exterior marked by the eclectic style of the late nineteenth century, even though inside it was a beautiful example of modern architecture in glass and steel—was reconsidered and supported by a forceful press campaign. At the time, Parisians were still reeling from the shock of the recent destruction of Les Halles, the food market that was a masterpiece of steel architecture from the 1850s. The idea of saving the train station dovetailed with the search by the museums and the Ministry of Culture for a site that would provide a dignified setting for Impressionist and Post-Impressionist painting. The container, in short, found its content. The decision dates from 1973; museographic programming began in 1978.

The adaptation of Victor Laloux's 1900 building, classified a historical monument, was entrusted to a trio of young architects—Renaud Bardon, Pierre Colboc, and Jean-Paul Philippon—and then, along with them, to Gae Aulenti for the fine tuning and overall appearance. The museum's team of curators in all disciplines—painting, sculpture, decorative arts, architecture, photography, and so on—led by Michel Laclotte (who, since the opening of the Orsay, has successfully overseen the completion of the Louvre's spectacular renovation and extension), began thinking together about appropriate uses for this train station. For all of us, deciding what should be chosen or eliminated, what the priorities should be and how the spaces should be organized was a difficult, passionate, often contentious process. What a challenge! On the very spot where trains came and went, at the site of so much commotion, of so many timetables and fleeting instants, were to be presented museum objects—which by their very nature aspire to eternity. In addition, permanent exhibition rooms had to be created without destroying the essence of an architectural structure that was itself a museum piece. Some of its main advantages were the immense glass vault overhead and the glass bays overlooking the Seine, diffusing northern light and, from the top floor, affording a marvelous view of Paris and its river.

Let's put aside the building for a moment and go inside the museum, which has been open to the public since December 1986. The period represented runs from 1848 to approximately 1905 for painting, and until 1914 for the rest. Why this time differential? Because pictorial developments generally preceded those of the other arts, displaying paintings made up to the start of World War I would have meant introducing to the Musée d'Orsay Fauvism, Cubism, and the beginnings of abstract art—basically a large part of the Beaubourg's domain and currently considered as belonging more to the beginning of the twentieth century than to the end of the nineteenth. This may, in fact, be open to debate. In any case, clear administrative boundaries had to be determined: thus, artists born between 1820 and 1870 are presented at the Musée d'Orsay; those born before that are in the Louvre, after that, at the Beaubourg. There are a few exceptions: the entire body of work by Edouard Vuillard, who was active until the 1940s, is at the Orsay, while the entire body of work by Henri Matisse, except for the one Neo-Impressionist painting reproduced here, is exhibited at the Beaubourg, even though he was born in 1869. As for Pierre Bonnard, his work is divided between the two institutions. Similarly, we did not wish to cut artists off from their immediate sources: thus, the tour of the museum begins with a few late works by Camille Corot, Eugène Delacroix, Jean-Auguste-Dominique

Ingres, François Rude, and Honoré Daumier, all of whom belong to the generation presented on the other side of the Seine, at the Louvre.

The dates 1848 and 1905, which in principle mark the beginning and end of the artistic creation shown here, may seem arbitrary boundaries, and a half-century of creation may seem a minor affair. But what a half-century it was! A time of such prodigious wealth and variety that the museum's eighteen thousand square meters of exhibition space barely suffice to contain it.

This mid-century corresponds, historically and culturally, to a moment of transition: it saw the appearance and recognition of Realism in the work of Gustave Courbet, Jean-François Millet, and the Barbizon landscape artists, as well as the first Universal Expositions (London, 1851; and Paris, 1855 and 1867). These world fairs disseminated European art and were a forum first for confrontation and eventually for association between art and industry, helping stimulate developments such as still photography and cinema. During this time, high-quality industrial art also emerged, conceived at first in England by groups of artist-artisans who were soon to be the creators of the Arts and Crafts movement. At the same time, new uses of steel were coming about that would rapidly transform architecture.

Such new tendencies faced increasing resistance from the eclectic, academic tradition, which would later be nicknamed "*art pompier.*" One of the particularities of the Musée d'Orsay is that it conveys these tensions and shows the variety of all these different modes of creation. Thus, the ground floor (the first part of the visit, ranging from 1848 to the 1870s, which more or less corresponds to the Second Empire in France) is divided in two by an alley of sculptures, ending in a sort of square dominated by the greatest French sculptor of the era, Jean-Baptiste Carpeaux. A series of models also evokes Baron Haussmann's new Paris and Charles Garnier's Opéra. On the right-hand side of this aisle is displayed work in the classical or academic current, featuring history painting, large decorative panels, and portraits, from Ingres and Delacroix to Pierre Puvis de Chavannes and the young Edgar Degas.

On the left, in opposition to Ingrism and Romanticism, are the social scenes and caricatures sculpted by Daumier, the Realism of the Barbizon landscape painters, and particularly the work of Courbet, whose large canvases, *Burial at Ornans* and *The Studio,* mark the beginning of a "new painting" even more than the famous Salon des Refusés of 1863. The hero of modernity in the 1860s, Edouard Manet, is represented opposite his friend Degas, who evolved out of the Ingres tradition but was also connected with the new generation of Claude Monet, Pierre-Auguste Renoir, Alfred Sisley, and Paul Cézanne—all future members of the Impressionist group. Work by these artists constitutes some of the museum's greatest highlights.

The second part of the painting tour takes the visitor behind the towers at the end of the aisle and onto the escalator to the upper gallery, where the glass roof diffuses the same fluctuating daylight that the Impressionists had made their subject. These artists are represented here in all their glory. After the masterpieces of the 1870s, each painter—Manet, Degas, Renoir, Monet, Cézanne—receives a comprehensive display.

Next comes another of the museum's most popular areas: beautiful series by

Vincent van Gogh, Paul Gauguin, and the Pont-Aven school; Georges Seurat and the Neo-Impressionists; Odilon Redon and Henri de Toulouse-Lautrec. After that section the visitor must go down to the middle floor to reach the exhibition spaces that open onto terraces filled with statues, ending in an esplanade devoted to the second great sculptor presented at the Musée d'Orsay: Auguste Rodin, with his *Gates of Hell* and *Balzac.*

To the left of the esplanade is a group of paintings that embodies the official and fashionable taste of the Third Republic, which preferred Léon Bonnat and William Bouguereau to Manet, and Ernest Meissonnier and Giovanni Boldini to Degas. Here we find famous portraits—from Albert Edelfelt's *Pasteur* to Jacques-Emile Blanche's *Proust,* as well as images that have filled the history books of several generations of young French students, such as Edouard Detaille's *Dream* and Jean-Paul Laurens's *Excommunication of Robert the Pious in 998.* Not far from here are works by foreign artists, often wisely acquired by the State at the time they were made. These include paintings by Winslow Homer, the Italian Pelizza di Volpedo, and the Russian Nikolai Nikolaievitch Gay. This section has been strengthened by additions made since the opening of the museum, enabling us to present artists such as Edward Burne-Jones (English), George Hendrik Breitner (Dutch), Ferdinand Hodler (Swiss), Gustav Klimt (Austrian), Edvard Munch (Norwegian), and Valentine Serov (Russian).

Finally, after the rooms devoted to decoration and to French and international Art Nouveau, in which decorative works by Redon and Bonnard are exhibited, the painting tour ends with works from the turn and early part of the twentieth century, including the Nabis—Maurice Denis, Félix Vallotton, Vuillard, and Bonnard—whom we observe here in their breathtaking maturity. It is Bonnard whose work fills the final room of the circuit, recently enriched by gifts.

While on this topic, let us not forget that the Musée d'Orsay would not exist without the donations and bequests that have been made since the end of the last century and that constitute the majority of the paintings on view here today. Let us briefly retrace these successive acts of generosity. First, that by the painter Gustave Caillebotte, whose bequest of 1896 put a great number of works by his Impressionist friends into the museums; by the Etienne Moreau-Nélatons, collectors who gave Manet's *Luncheon on the Grass* and an excellent selection of Impressionist paintings (1906); by Isaac de Camondo, who, in particular, brought Cézanne into the Louvre and gave Manet's *Balcony* as well as a superb series of works by Degas (1911). Let us also recall the bequests of Chauchard (1909), who gave the state Millet's famous *Angelus* and an exceptional collection of landscape works from the Barbizon School. We should mention particularly the postwar donations by Dr. Paul Gachet and by his son (seven Cézannes and as many van Goghs) (1949-54), by Eduardo Mollard (1961) and by Max and Rosy Kaganovitch (1973), not to mention Auguste Pellerin's bequest of several works by Cézanne, followed by his family's donation of that artist's *Woman with a Coffee Pot* (1956). Masterpieces have also been left to us by Jacques Doucet (1929) and John Quinn (1927): Henri Rousseau's *Snake Charmer* and Seurat's *Circus,* respectively.

The artists' descendants, too, have allowed works by Frédéric Bazille, Courbet,

Degas, Emile Gallé, Monet, Camille Pissarro, Redon, Renoir, Paul Sérusier, Paul Signac, Toulouse-Lautrec, and others to be displayed or better represented. The same generosity has been evident, in the area of portraiture, among the models and their families: this is the source, for example, of Manet's *Zola*, of Franz-Xaver Winterhalter's *Madame Barbe de Rimsky-Korsakov*, of Jules-Elie Delaunay's *Madame Georges Bizet*, of van Gogh's *Dr. Paul Gachet*, of Serov's *Mme. Lvov*, of Louis Welden Hawkins's *Séverine*, and of Bonnard's *Portrait of the Bernheim Brothers*—to cite only those that are reproduced here.

Ever since the principle of *dation*—using works of art for the payment of inheritance taxes—was instituted in France in 1968, numerous masterpieces have thus been acquired: works by Manet (*The Escape of Rochefort*), Monet (*Luncheon on the Grass* and *Rue Montorgueil, Paris: Festival of June 30, 1878*), Renoir (*Dance in the City*), Bonnard (*The Seasons, The Loge, The Bourgeois Afternoon*), Redon (*Decorative Panels*), and Matisse (*Luxe, calme et volupté*).

We should perhaps note where all the works now exhibited at the Musée d'Orsay were originally housed. To simplify matters: whatever is prior to Impressionism had been at the Louvre, either exhibited (Courbet, for example) or in storage (many academic works). Works by Manet, the Impressionists, and the immediate Post-Impressionists (van Gogh, Gauguin, Seurat) had been exhibited at the Jeu de Paume. Painting from after this period—the Nabis, Symbolists, foreign schools, and so on—had been on display or in storage at the Musée National d'Art Moderne before being transferred to the Beaubourg. Just about everything else now on view at the Musée d'Orsay was not being displayed anywhere. Many of the sculptures were in storage or otherwise inaccessible at the Louvre, except those by Carpeaux and Rodin (the Rodin museum has generously entrusted us with certain of its pieces). As with painting, we have endeavored to show the variety of sculpture from the Second Empire to the end of the century: from Auguste Préault's and Jean-Paul Aubé's Romanticism, to Daumier's and then Jules Dalou's Realism and to the various forms of the classicist revival, from Albert-Ernest Carrier-Belleuse in mid-century to Aristide Maillol and Emile-Antoine Bourdelle at the turn of this century. We go from the eclectic style of classical practitioners such as Charles Cordier and Louis-Ernest Barrias—who played with materials by mixing marble, semiprecious stones, and bronze—to the technical innovations or return to primitivism by painter-sculptors such as Degas and Gauguin.

Since the museum's mandate is to present a multidisciplinary view of this half-century, we have had to attempt to fill in entire areas of creation that had previously been absent from the national collections. Indeed, aside from a few loans from the Musée des Arts Décoratifs, everything now on display at the Musée d'Orsay in the area of furnishings, objets d'art, architecture, and photography has been acquired over the last fifteen years.

The furniture and objets d'art are divided into two main sections. On the ground floor, to the right of the painting circuit, are the rooms devoted to the Second Empire—its wallpapers, the wealth of its gold and cabinet work, the technical refinement of its everyday objects, and several masterpieces of the eclectic neo-Greek and neo-Gothic styles. With few exceptions, we have avoided mixing disciplines or combining paintings, sculptures, and objects from the same period in one room; there is no "period room" at the Musée d'Orsay, no reconstructed atmosphere. On first glance when entering the museum, the sight of all the sculptures in perspective under the great glass vault may evoke not a specific interior but the style of the Salon exhibitions at the nineteenth-century Expositions Universelles. Painting, here as in the Salons, unfolds in separate galleries, but the whole does not seek to imitate a plush, hothouse effect; on the contrary, the space is defined by the strong contemporary architecture of Gae Aulenti, who emphasized the transparent, metallic structure of Laloux's train station.

The second section of furniture and objets d'art, which is devoted to the international modernist decorative arts of the end of the century—called Art Nouveau, Jugendstil, or modern style—is situated on the second floor and in the upper pavilion. Here we find the pioneers of English design beginning in the 1860s–70s, followed by creators as inventive as Hector Guimard, Emile Gallé, and René-Jules Lalique (France); Henry Van de Velde (Belgium); Charles Rennie Mackintosh (Scotland); Josef Hoffmann and Koloman Moser (Austria); Carlo Bugatti (Italy); and Frank Lloyd Wright (United States).

Many of these creators were architects, a domain that is also represented in the museum by models and drawings, plans, re-creations, and other projects, a selection of which gives one a sense of the period's variety, from the eclecticism of the Second Empire and the visionary or traditionalist Beaux-Arts style to industrial architecture and Art Nouveau. To protect them from the damaging effects of light, architectural drawings are shown only in rotation, as are all the other drawings, to which several rooms are devoted. To the Orsay's wonderful collection of nineteenth-century drawings and watercolors, stored at the Cabinet des Arts Graphiques in the Musée du Louvre, has recently been added a series of gifts or acquisitions of works by Charles Baudelaire, Degas, Gauguin, and Seurat, several of which have been selected for inclusion here. Whereas these works on paper cannot be permanently exhibited, the same is not true of the famous pastels by Millet, Manet, and Redon reproduced here, which are kept on display under very faint lighting.

The fragility of photographic paper means that our collection, which is extremely rich, is displayed only for short periods. One should not be surprised, therefore, to find works in this book that might not be seen in the course of one's visit in person. The photographic collection has been established over the last fifteen years with an eye to diversity and internationalism, as evidenced here by a choice that ranges from early specimens of photography—daguerreotypes or negatives on paper from the years 1840–50 by William Henry Fox Talbot, Charles Nègre, Gustave Le Gray, Nadar, and Lewis Carroll—to the most modern examples by Eugène Atget and Edward Steichen.

In conclusion, I would like to express the wish that *Treasures of the Musée d'Orsay* will help the reader preserve vivid memories of the quality and the variety of works seen at this museum. May it especially instill a desire to return again and again in search of new discoveries.

CLASSICISM

"Classicism" defines any art that is founded on admiration of antiquity. The nineteenth century came to be known as the "history century," with its artists capable of admiring and seeking inspiration from all time periods, but it began by declaring itself heir to late eighteenth-century Neoclassicism and the quest for a timeless ideal.

The lofty figure of Jean-Auguste-Dominique Ingres dominates this current. A product of Jacques-Louis David's studio, he later became director of the French Academy in Rome, and a large part of his life was spent in voluntary exile. Ingres's art, far from being solely academic, played a role in the development of artistic modernity, as evidenced by the "Ingrisms" of Edgar Degas, Pierre-Auguste Renoir, and Pablo Picasso, and by Pop Art's many tributes to him. The anatomical distortions that Ingres brought to his figures have often been noted, and their strangeness or archaism have prompted remarks such as Théodore Silvestre's comment that Ingres was a "Chinese painter lost in the mid-nineteenth century among the Athenian ruins." Though a believer in the traditional hierarchy of painting types, the pinnacle of which was "history" painting (the narrative portrayal of a noble subject), Ingres is most celebrated for his portraits and nudes: *Venus at Paphos* (page 16) shows how the painter was able to create a paradoxical eroticism from an incomplete portrait transformed into a nude.

Ingres's formal research did not lend itself to the formation of a school. His collaborators themselves (Amaury-Duval, Hippolyte Flandrin) seem to have been disciples more than students. Théodore Chassériau moved harmoniously from Ingres's teachings into Eugène Delacroix's orbit. Other artists made other transitions: Thomas Couture, whose *The Romans of the Decadence* (opposite and page 18) was intended as a compromise between Classicism and Romanticism, initiated the eclecticism that his student Edouard Manet was able to expand upon; Pierre Puvis de Chavannes, the father of Symbolism, invented a decorative painting in the full sense of the word, a concept that others, including the Nabis, would later adopt.

Detail of Thomas Couture, *The Romans of the Decadence,* 1847. See page 18.

RIGHT Jean-Auguste-Dominique Ingres
(1780–1867).
Venus at Paphos, 1852–53.
Oil on canvas,
36 x 27⅝ in. (91 x 70 cm).

BELOW Jean-Auguste-Dominique Ingres
(1780–1867).
The Virgin with the Host, 1854.
Oil on canvas,
diameter: 44 in. (113 cm).

OPPOSITE Jean-Auguste-Dominique Ingres
(1780–1867).
The Spring, 1856.
Oil on canvas,
64½ x 31½ in. (163 x 80 cm).
Bequest of the comtesse Duchâtel,
to the Louvre, 1878.

ABOVE Thomas Couture (1815–1879).
The Romans of the Decadence, 1847.
Oil on canvas,
15½ ft. x 25 ft. 3⅝ in. (4.72 x 7.72 m).

BELOW Théodore Chassériau (1819–1856).
"The Tepidarium," 1853.
Oil on canvas,
67⅜ x 101⅝ in. (171 x 258 cm).

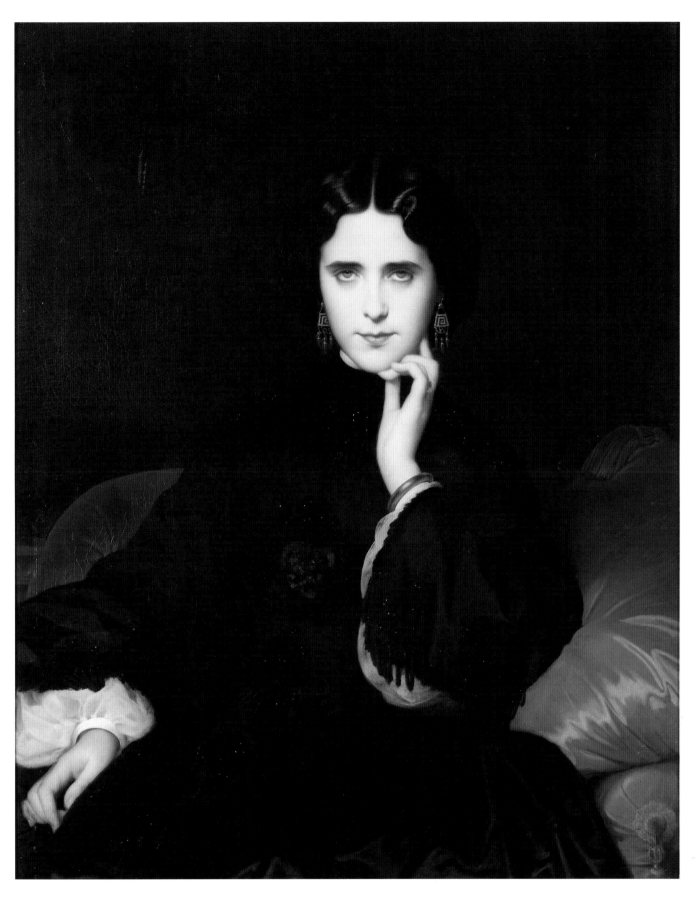

Amaury-Duval (1808–1885).
Madame de Loynes, 1862.
Oil on canvas,
39⅜ x 32⅝ in. (100 x 83 cm).

ABOVE Pierre Puvis de Chavannes
(1824–1898).
Hope, c. 1872.
Oil on canvas,
27⅝ x 32⅜ in. (70 x 82 cm).

BELOW Pierre Puvis de Chavannes
(1824–1898).
The Poor Fisherman, 1881.
Oil on canvas,
61 x 75⅝ in. (155 x 192 cm).

Pierre Puvis de Chavannes (1824–1898).
Young Girls at the Seaside, 1879.
Oil on canvas,
80⅝ x 60⅝ in. (205 x 154 cm).
Gift of Robert Gérard, 1970.

ROMANTICISM
AND REALISM

The best symbol of Romanticism remains Eugène Delacroix's sketch for *The Lion Hunt* (page 24). For Charles Baudelaire, writing in 1846, Romanticism was "the most recent, the most current expression of the beautiful"; with it was born a modernity that he defined as "the transitory, the fugitive, the contingent, half-art, the other half of which is the eternal and the immutable."

The revolution of 1848 (which inspired Honoré Daumier's *Republic,* page 24, painted for a competition organized by the new government) marked the moment when, in literature as in painting, Romanticism tipped into Realism. In 1855 the second Exposition Universelle took place in Paris: a large part of its attraction rested in the confrontation of works by Jean-Auguste-Dominique Ingres with those by Delacroix. At the same time Gustave Courbet exhibited *The Painter's Studio* (page 30) and other works in his "Pavilion of Realism," isolated on the avenue Montaigne. As he wrote in his *Manifesto of Realism:* "I simply wanted to draw the reasoned and independent feeling of my own individuality from complete knowledge of the tradition. To know in order to be able to do, this was my thought."

One of Courbet's innovations consisted in painting "trivial" subjects in large formats, conferring dignity on modern subjects in order to compete with history painting. Realist themes often focused on social analysis, initially of the peasant world. The entire political gamut was eventually represented, from social conservatism (in 1859, Emperor Napoleon III bought Jules Breton's *The Calling in of the Gleaners,* page 32) to progressivism.

In the case of landscape painting, diverse movements were even more closely intertwined. Within Orientalism, periods of work that was "all imagination," according to Eugène Fromentin, and of work that was "all observation" followed one another. Delacroix found an antiquity alive and well in the Orient, while Camille Corot in Rome produced modern versions of the classical landscape, reviving the pastoral scene. The pantheist Théodore Rousseau exemplified a barely perceptible passage from Romanticism to the Barbizon school, whose other members included Charles-François Daubigny and Jean-François Millet. The principle of the latter, which was to paint from nature, was soon to be adopted by the Impressionists Frédéric Bazille and Claude Monet, who were also active in Barbizon.

Detail of Camille Corot, *The Artist's Studio, Young Woman with a Mandolin,* c. 1865. See page 26.

Eugène Delacroix (1798–1863).
The Lion Hunt (sketch), 1854.
Oil on canvas,
33⅞ x 45⅜ in. (86 x 115 cm).

Honoré Daumier (1808–1879).
The Republic (sketch), 1848.
Oil on canvas,
28⅝ x 23⅝ in. (73 x 60 cm).
Gift of Etienne Moreau-Nélaton, 1906.

Honoré Daumier (1808–1879).
The Laundress, 1863.
Oil on wood,
19⅜ x 13 in. (49 x 33 cm).
Acquired with the assistance of
M. David-Weill, 1927.

Camille Corot (1796–1875).
The Artist's Studio, Young Woman
with a Mandolin, c. 1865.
Oil on canvas,
22⅛ x 18⅛ in. (56 x 46 cm).
Acquired with the assistance of
Mme. Hubert Morand, 1933.

Rosa Bonheur (1822–1899).
Ploughing in the Nivernais Region, 1849.
Oil on canvas,
52¾ x 102⅜ in. (134 x 260 cm).

Charles-François Daubigny (1817–1878).
Harvest, 1851.
Oil on canvas,
53⅛ x 77¼ in. (135 x 196 cm).

Gustave Courbet (1819–1877).
Burial at Ornans, 1849–50.
Oil on canvas,
10 ft. 3½ in. x 21 ft. 11 in. (3.15 x 6.68 m).
Gift of Juliette Courbet,
sister of the artist, 1881.

Gustave Courbet (1819–1877).
*The Painter's Studio: Allegory of Seven Years
of My Artistic and Moral Life,* 1854–55.
Oil on canvas,
11 ft. 9⅝ in. x 19 ft. 7¼ in. (3.61 x 5.98 m).
Acquired with the assistance of a
public subscription and the Société des
Amis du Louvre, 1920.

ABOVE Gustave Courbet (1819–1877).
The Wounded Man, 1844–54.
Oil on canvas,
31⅞ x 38¼ in. (81 x 97 cm).

BELOW Gustave Courbet (1819–1877).
The Wave, 1870.
Oil on canvas,
46⅛ x 63 in. (117 x 160 cm).

ABOVE Jules Breton (1827–1906).
The Calling in of the Gleaners, 1859.
Oil on canvas,
35⅜ x 69⅜ in. (90 x 176 cm).
Acquired by the Civil List of
Napoleon III, 1859.

BELOW Jean-François Millet (1814–1875).
The Gleaners, 1857.
Oil on canvas,
32⅝ x 43⅝ in. (83 x 111 cm).
Gift of Mme. Pommery, 1890.

Jean-François Millet (1814–1875).
The Angelus, 1857–59.
Oil on canvas,
21⅝ x 26 in. (55 x 66 cm).
Bequest of Alfred Chauchard, 1909.

ABOVE Eugène Boudin (1824–1898).
Bathers on the Beach at Trouville, 1869.
Oil on wood,
12¼ x 18⅞ in. (31 x 48 cm).
Bequest of the comte
Isaac de Camondo, 1911.

BELOW Gustave Doré (1832–1883).
The Enigma, 1871.
Oil on canvas,
51¼ x 76¾ in. (130 x 195 cm).

Gustave Moreau (1826–1898).
Orpheus, 1865.
Oil on wood,
60⅝ x 39 in. (154 x 99 cm).

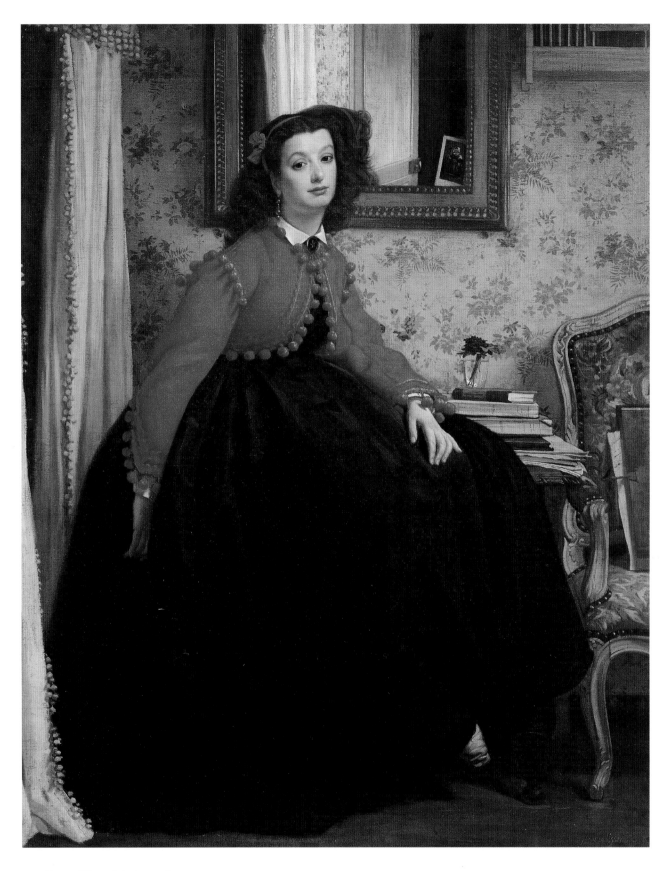

James Tissot (1836–1902).
Portrait of Mlle. L. L., or
Young Woman in a Red Jacket, 1864.
Oil on canvas,
48¾ x 39 in. (124 x 99 cm).

Alfred Stevens (1823–1906).
The Bath, c. 1867.
Oil on canvas,
29⅛ x 36⅝ in. (74 x 93 cm).
Bequest of the painter
Léon Lhermitte, 1926.

HISTORY PAINTING AND OFFICIAL PORTRAITS

Starting in the eighteenth century and continuing through the nineteenth, the Salons (exhibitions held by the Académie Royale de Peinture et de Sculpture) became one of the main events of public artistic life in Paris. The works were selected by a jury that, after the First Empire, was made up exclusively of members of the Académie. Because the academic style was considered "rational," it could be transmitted from teacher to student, and painters followed a highly regulated curriculum that included study at the Ecole des Beaux-Arts in Paris and, for a select few, at the Villa Medici in Rome.

One example of the perpetuation of tradition through education is François-Edouard Picot, a student of Jacques-Louis David's who was famous for his teaching and for his decorations of Parisian churches. First in his studio and then at the Beaux-Arts, Picot trained future prizewinners in painting, including not only Paul Baudry, Alexandre Cabanel, and William Bouguereau but also Gustave Guillaumet and even Gustave Moreau.

There were other, sometimes surprising points of contact that enabled innovative artists to prepare for future battle through exposure to traditional milieux: Charles Gleyre's studio, a kind of preparatory class for the Beaux-Arts, was attended by Claude Monet, Pierre-Auguste Renoir, and Alfred Sisley; Edgar Degas, Eugène Delacroix, and Moreau were all students at the Beaux-Arts. In addition, there were private courses at the Académie Julian, from which the Nabis and Henri Matisse emerged, and at the Académie Suisse.

The "historical" subjects presented in this chapter, which were sometimes taken to unexpected heights (see, for example, Edouard Detaille's *Dream,* page 46), are complemented by a variety of portraits. These range from the man of science (*Louis Pasteur,* page 47) to the fin-de-siècle dandy Robert de Montesquiou (page 49)—who inspired the Baron de Charlus in Marcel Proust's *Remembrance of Things Past,* as well as Oscar Wilde's Dorian Gray and Joris-Karl Huysmans's Des Esseintes.

Detail of Ernest Meissonier, *Campaign in France, 1814,* 1864. See page 42.

Franz-Xaver Winterhalter (1805–1873).
Madame Barbe de Rimsky-Korsakov, 1864.
Oil on canvas,
46⅛ x 35⅜ in. (117 x 90 cm).
Gift of Nicolas and Dmitry Rimskky-
Korsakow, sons of the model, 1879.

Carolus-Duran (1837–1917).
Lady with a Glove, 1869.
Oil on canvas,
89¾ x 64⅝ in. (228 x 164 cm).

Ernest Meissonier (1815–1891).
Campaign in France, 1814, 1864.
Oil on wood,
20⅛ x 29⅞ in. (51 x 76 cm).
Bequest of Alfred Chauchard, 1909.

ABOVE Alexandre Cabanel (1823–1889).
*The Death of Francesca da Rimini and
Paolo Malatesta,* 1870.
Oil on canvas,
72⅜ x 100¾ in. (184 x 255 cm).

BELOW Jean-Paul Laurens (1838–1921).
*The Excommunication of
Robert the Pious in 998,* 1875.
Oil on canvas,
51¼ x 85¾ in. (130 x 218 cm).

Léon Bonnat (1833–1922).
Madame Pasca, 1874.
Oil on canvas,
87⅜ x 52 in. (222 x 132 cm).

William Bouguereau (1825–1905).
The Birth of Venus, 1879.
Oil on canvas,
118⅛ x 84⅝ in. (300 x 215 cm).

ABOVE Edouard Detaille (1848–1912).
The Dream, 1888.
Oil on canvas,
9 ft. 10 in. x 13 ft. 1¼ in. (3 x 4 m).

BELOW Henri Gervex (1852–1929).
A Painting Jury, 1885.
Oil on canvas,
9 ft. 9⅝ in. x 13 ft. 8⅜ in. (2.99 x 4.19 m).
Gift of Pierre Waldeck-Rousseau, 1892.

Albert Edelfelt (1854–1905).
Louis Pasteur, 1885.
Oil on canvas,
60⅝ x 49⅝ in. (154 x 126 cm).

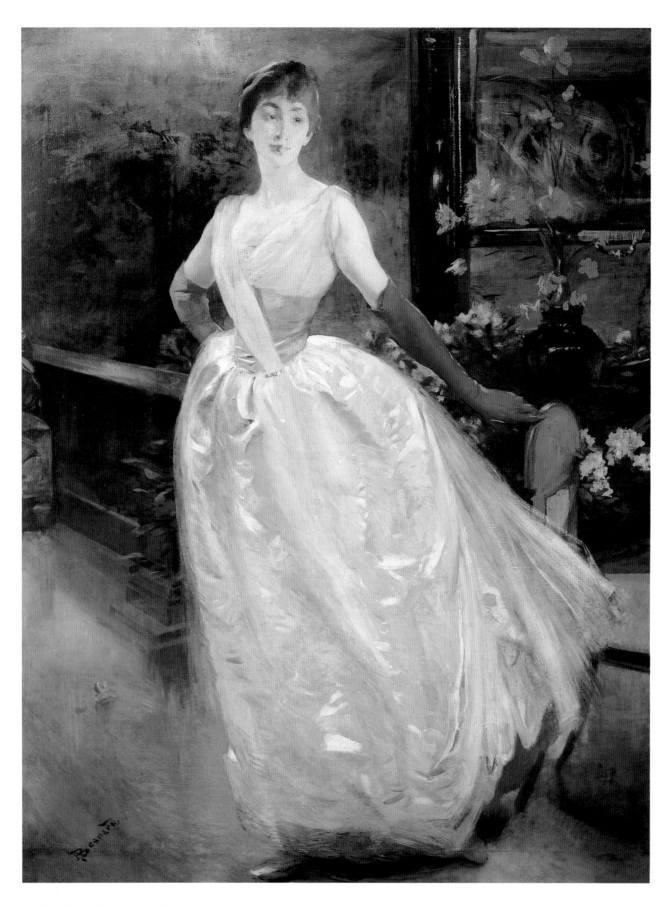

Albert Besnard (1849–1934).
Madame Roger Jourdain, 1886.
Oil on canvas,
78⅝ x 60¼ in. (200 x 153 cm).
Gift of Mme. Roger Jourdain,
the model, 1921.

Giovanni Boldini (1842–1931).
Count Robert de Montesquiou, 1897.
Oil on canvas,
63 x 32⅜ in. (160 x 82 cm).
Gift of Henri Pinard in honor of the
comte Robert de Montesquiou, 1922.

THE NEW PAINTING OF THE
1860s AND IMPRESSIONISM

R ejection from the Salons appears, in retrospect, to have been a catalyst for the conception of a new style of painting. In 1863, faced with a controversy caused by the rejection of numerous works by the Salon jury, Napoleon III created the Salon des Refusés, whose scandal over Edouard Manet's *Luncheon on the Grass* (opposite and page 52) was amplified, two years later at the official Salon, by outrage over his *Olympia* (page 53).

Similarly, again in response to the rejection of their works by the Salon, a group of painters (derisively baptized "Impressionists") organized eight independent exhibitions between 1874 and 1886. Although Manet never participated in their shows, he drew nearer to the group's aesthetic after the Franco-Prussian War of 1870. The aesthetic unity within the group seems to have been compromised as early as the 1879 exhibition, and after 1880 Paul Cézanne, who was represented in the initial exhibitions, distanced himself from the group.

There were profound differences in the work of these artists. Strictly speaking, the "pure" Impressionism of Pierre-Auguste Renoir, Claude Monet, Camille Pissarro, and Alfred Sisley marked the culmination of the endeavor to render a modern vision of the ephemeral by recording the transitory aspect of light, an endeavor well suited to working in series. But these works have little in common with those by, say, Edgar Degas, whose compositions are oriented toward a kind of choreography that became openly theatrical in *In a Café* (also known as *The Absinthe Drinker,* page 62). And what did any of these have in common with the "sensation" sought by Cézanne, who undertook to "treat nature through the cylinder, the sphere and the cone"?

Beginning in 1880, the "pure" Impressionists were concerned with producing a more constructed art; Pissarro, for example, embarked on a Pointillist phase. Each pursued a solitary evolution, sometimes late in his career, as in the cases of Renoir and Monet. Did they share the desire expressed by Cézanne to make Impressionism into "something solid and lasting, like the art in museums"?

Despite the incomprehension of the public and sometimes even of their sympathizers, the Impressionists had support from collectors like Jean-Baptiste Faure and dealers like Paul Durand-Ruel. One who went on to support subsequent generations was Ambroise Vollard, who was dealer first to Manet and Cézanne, then eventually to Henri Rousseau, Henri Matisse, and Pablo Picasso.

Detail of Edouard Manet, *Luncheon on the Grass,* 1863. See page 52.

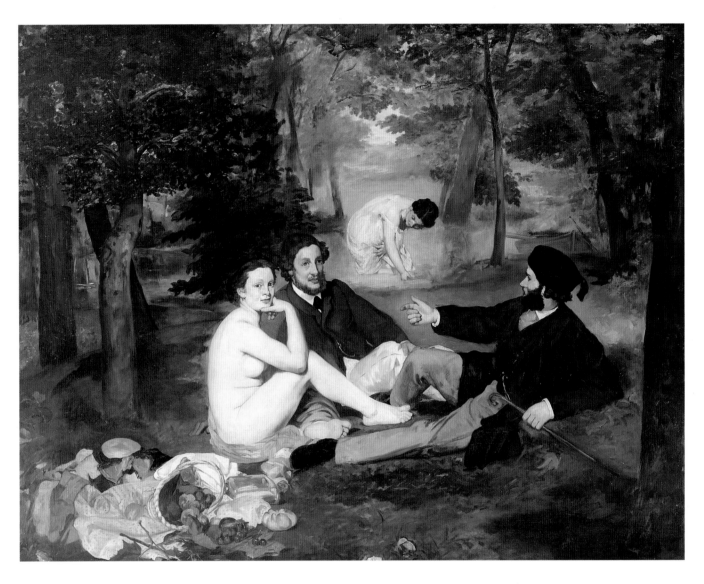

Edouard Manet (1832–1883).
Luncheon on the Grass, 1863.
Oil on canvas,
81⅞ x 103⅞ in. (208 x 264 cm).
Gift of Etienne Moreau-Nélaton, 1906.

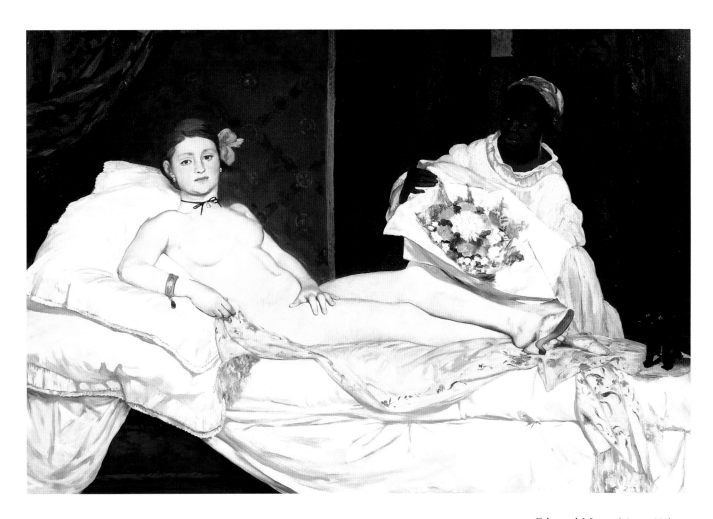

Edouard Manet (1832–1883).
Olympia, 1863.
Oil on canvas,
51¼ x 74¾ in. (130 x 190 cm).
Offered to the state by public
subscription through the initiative
of Claude Monet, 1890.

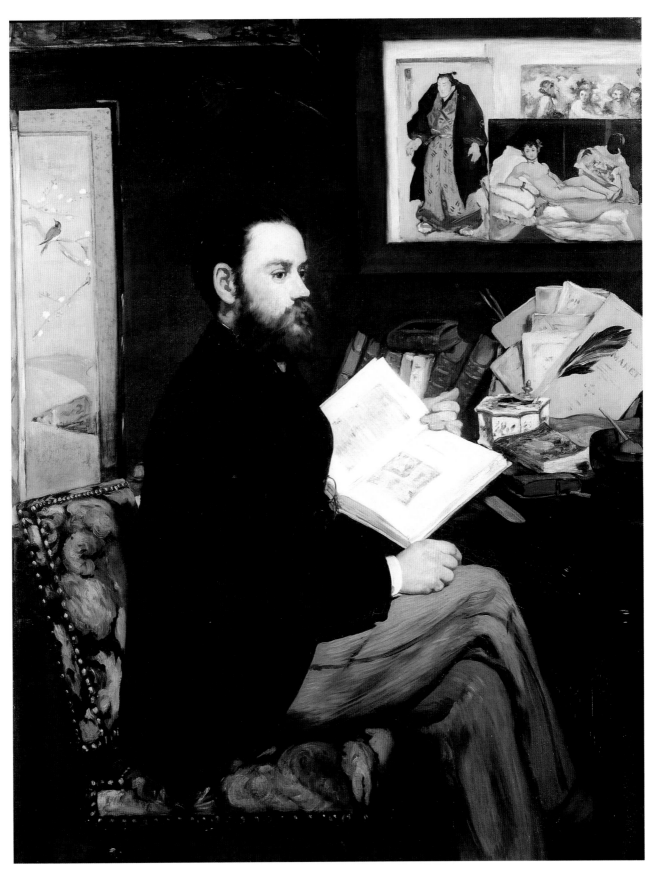

OPPOSITE Edouard Manet (1832–1883).
The Fife Player, 1866.
Oil on canvas,
63⅜ x 38¼ in. (161 x 97 cm).
Bequest of the comte
Isaac de Camondo, 1911.

ABOVE Edouard Manet (1832–1883).
Emile Zola, 1868.
Oil on canvas,
57½ x 44⅞ in. (146 x 114 cm).
Gift of Mme. Emile Zola, 1918.

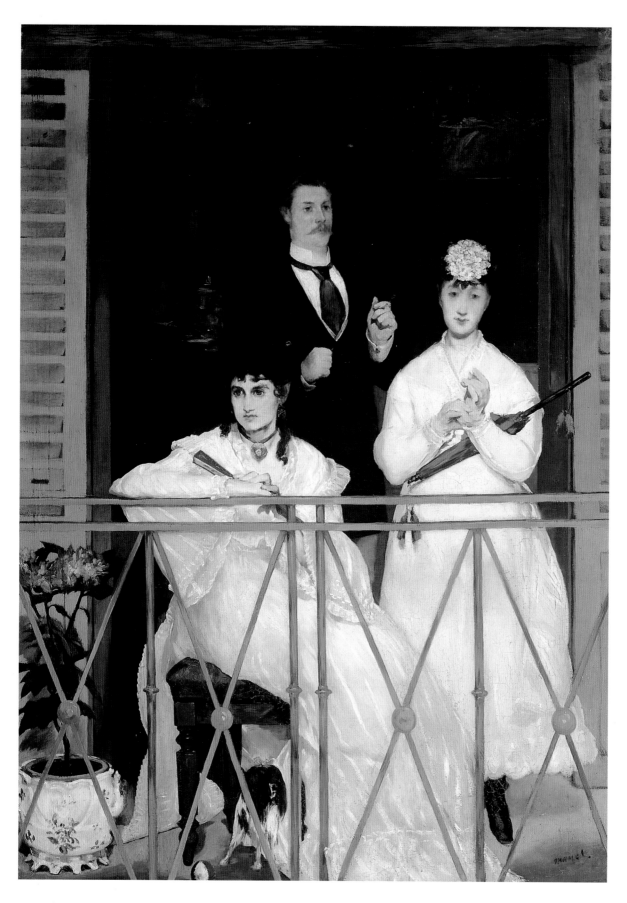

Edouard Manet (1832–1883).
The Balcony, 1868–69.
Oil on canvas,
66⅞ x 48¾ in. (170 x 124 cm).
Bequest of Gustave Caillebotte, 1894.

ABOVE Edouard Manet (1832–1883).
On the Beach, 1873.
Oil on canvas,
23¼ x 28¾ in. (59 x 73 cm).
Gift of Jean-Edouard Dubrujeaud, 1953.

BELOW Edouard Manet (1832–1883).
Stéphane Mallarmé, 1876.
Oil on canvas,
10⅝ x 14¼ in. (27 x 36 cm).

Edgar Degas (1834–1917).
The Bellelli Family, 1858–67.
Oil on canvas,
78⅝ x 98⅜ in. (200 x 250 cm).

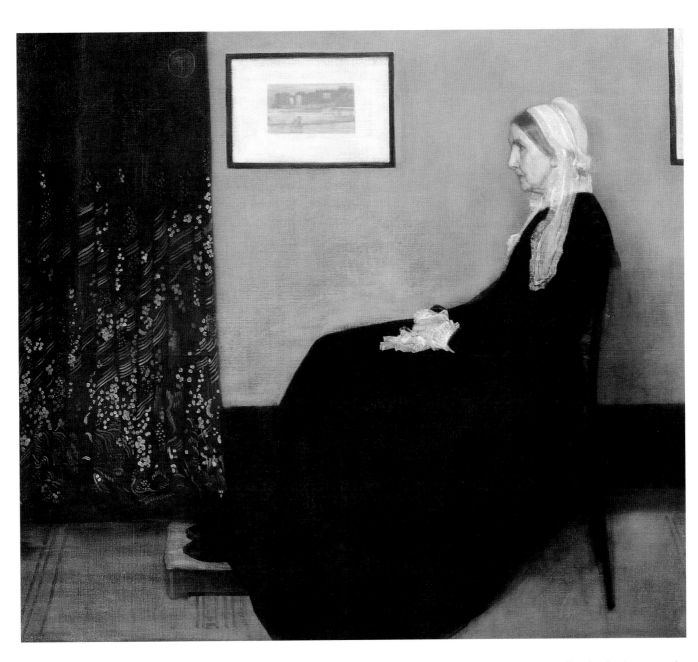

James McNeill Whistler (1834–1903).
Arrangement in Grey and Black, No. 1,
or *The Artist's Mother,* 1871.
Oil on canvas,
56⅝ x 63¾ in. (144 x 162 cm).

ABOVE Edgar Degas (1834–1917).
Racehorses in Front of the Grandstand,
c. 1866–68.
Oil on paper on canvas,
18½ x 24 in. (46 x 61 cm).
Bequest of the comte
Isaac de Camondo, 1911.

BELOW Edgar Degas (1834–1917).
The Dance Class at the Opéra,
rue Le Peletier, 1872.
Oil on canvas,
12⅝ x 18⅛ in. (32 x 46 cm).
Bequest of the comte
Isaac de Camondo, 1911.

Edgar Degas (1834–1917).
The Dance Class, c. 1873–76.
Oil on canvas,
33½ x 29½ in. (85 x 75 cm).
Bequest of the comte
Isaac de Camondo, 1911.

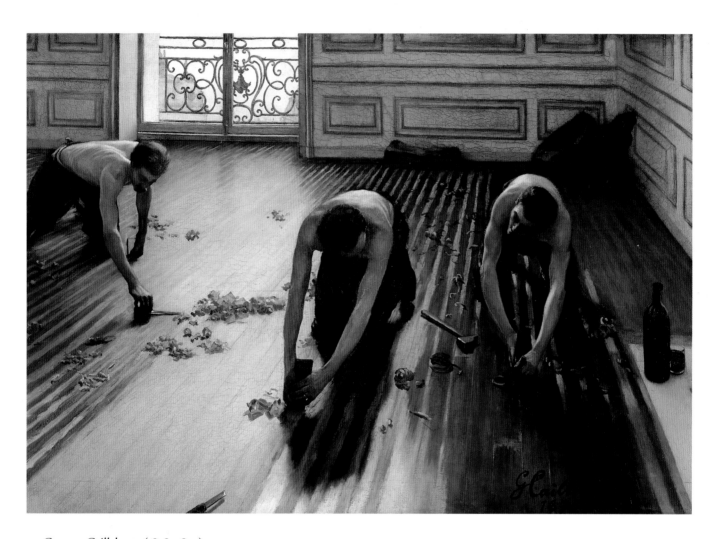

Gustave Caillebotte (1848–1894).
The Floor Scrapers, 1875.
Oil on canvas,
40⅛ x 57⅜ in. (102 x 146 cm).
Gift of the heirs of Gustave Caillebotte
through the intervention of
Auguste Renoir, 1894.

ABOVE Henri Fantin-Latour (1836–1904).
Corner of the Table, 1872.
Oil on canvas,
62⅞ x 88½ in. (160 x 225 cm).
Gift of M. and Mme. Blémont, 1910.

BELOW Frédéric Bazille (1841–1870).
The Artist's Studio, 1870.
Oil on canvas,
38⅝ x 50⅜ in. (98 x 128 cm).
Bequest of Marc Bazille, brother of
the artist, 1924.

Claude Monet (1840–1926).
Luncheon on the Grass, 1865–66.
Oil on canvas,
97⅝ x 85⅜ in. (248 x 217 cm).
Acquired by *dation,* 1987;
formerly the Eknayan Collection.

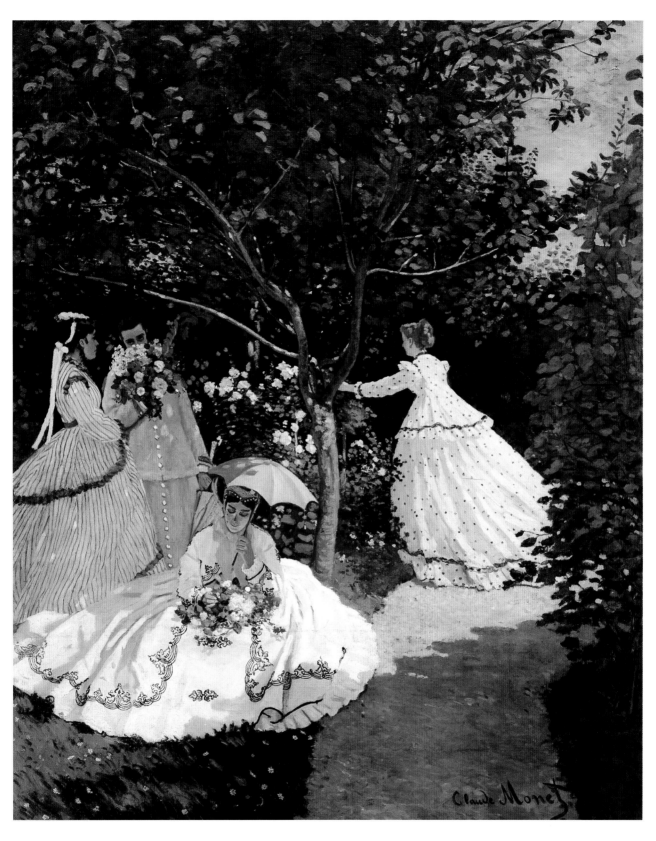

Claude Monet (1840–1926).
Women in a Garden, 1867.
Oil on canvas,
100⅜ x 80⅝ in. (255 x 205 cm).

ABOVE Claude Monet (1840–1926).
Argenteuil Basin, c. 1872.
Oil on canvas,
23⅝ x 31½ in. (60 x 80 cm).
Bequest of the comte
Isaac de Camondo, 1944.

BELOW Claude Monet (1840–1926).
Poppies, 1873.
Oil on canvas,
19⅝ x 25⅝ in. (50 x 65 cm).
Gift of Etienne Moreau-Nélaton, 1906.

Claude Monet (1840–1926).
Saint-Lazare Station, 1877.
Oil on canvas,
29½ x 40⅞ in. (75 x 104 cm).
Bequest of Gustave Caillebotte, 1894.

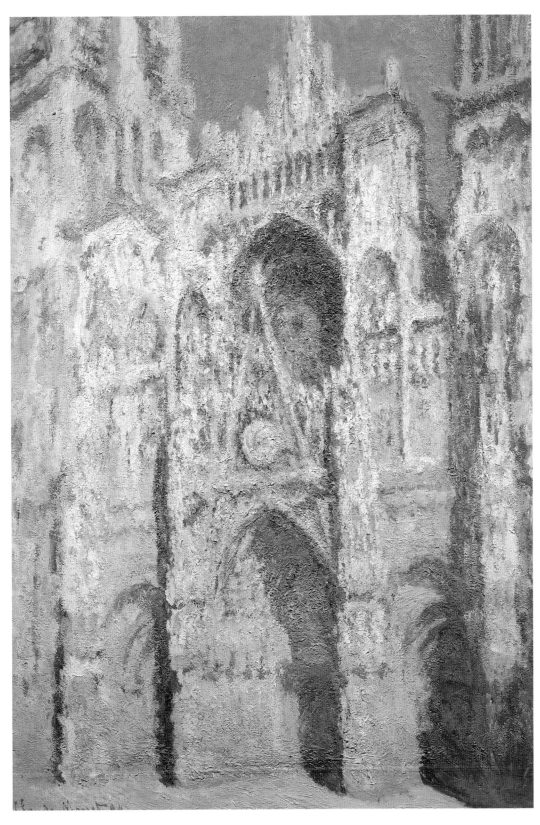

ABOVE Claude Monet (1840–1926).
*Rouen Cathedral: The Portal and
the Saint-Romain Tower in Full Sun,
Harmony in Blue and Gold*, 1893.
Oil on canvas,
42⅛ x 28⅝ in. (107 x 73 cm).
Bequest of the comte
Isaac de Camondo, 1911.

OPPOSITE Claude Monet (1840–1926).
*Rue Montorgueil, Paris:
Festival of June 30, 1878*, 1878.
Oil on canvas,
31⅞ x 19⅝ in. (81 x 50 cm).
Acquired by *dation*, 1982.

Claude Monet (1840–1926).
*Woman with Parasol Turned
toward the Left,* 1886.
Oil on canvas,
51⅝ x 34⅝ in. (131 x 88 cm).
Gift of Michel Monet,
son of the artist, 1927.

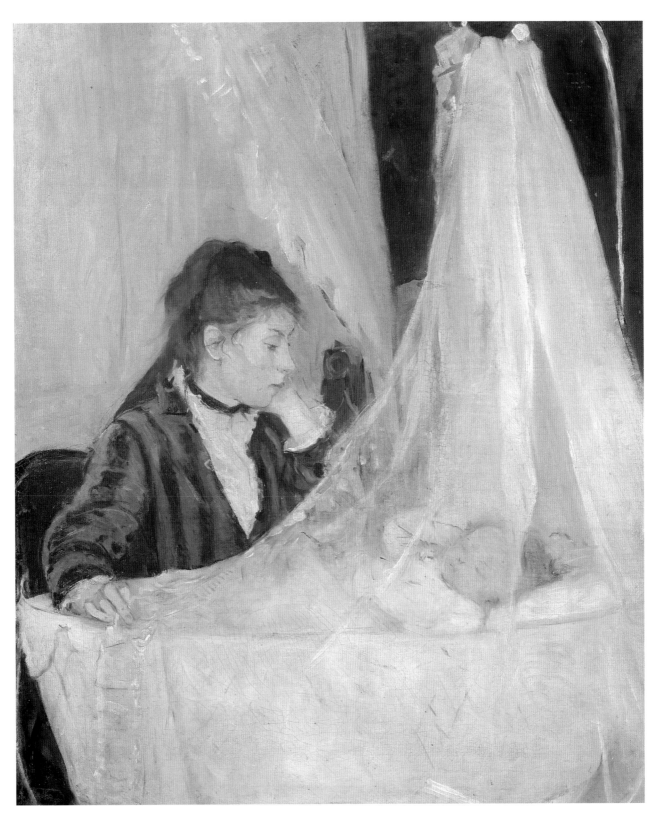

Berthe Morisot (1841–1895).
The Cradle, 1872.
Oil on canvas,
22⅛ x 18⅛ in. (56 x 46 cm).

Camille Pissarro
(1830–1903).
Self-Portrait, 1873.
Oil on canvas,
22⅛ x 18⅛ in. (56 x 46 cm).
Gift of Paul-Emile Pissarro,
son of the artist, 1930.

ABOVE Camille Pissarro (1830–1903).
*The Entrance to the Village
of Voisins*, 1872.
Oil on canvas,
18⅛ x 21⅝ in. (46 x 55 cm).
Gift of Ernest May, 1923.

BELOW Camille Pissarro (1830–1903).
*Red Roofs, a Corner of the
Village in Winter*, 1877.
Oil on canvas,
21⅜ x 25⅝ in. (54 x 65 cm).
Bequest of Gustave Caillebotte, 1894.

Pierre-Auguste Renoir (1841–1919).
The Swing, 1876.
Oil on canvas,
36¼ x 28⅝ in. (92 x 73 cm).
Bequest of Gustave Caillebotte, 1894.

Pierre-Auguste Renoir (1841–1919).
Dance at the Moulin de la Galette,
Montmartre, 1876.
Oil on canvas,
51⅝ x 68⅞ in. (131 x 175 cm).
Bequest of Gustave Caillebotte, 1894.

Pierre-Auguste Renoir (1841–1919).
Young Girl, Seated, c. 1909.
Oil on canvas,
25⅝ x 21⅜ in. (65 x 54 cm).
Bequest of the comte
Isaac de Camondo, 1911.

Pierre-Auguste Renoir (1841–1919).
Bathers, c. 1918–19.
Oil on canvas,
43⅜ x 63 in. (110 x 160 cm).
Gift of the artist's sons, 1923.

ABOVE Alfred Sisley (1839–1899).
Chemin de la Machine, Louveciennes, 1873.
Oil on canvas,
21⅝ x 28⅝ in. (54 x 73 cm).
Gift of Joanny Peytel, 1914.

BELOW Alfred Sisley (1839–1899).
The Boat During the Flood, 1876.
Oil on canvas,
19⅝ x 24 in. (50 x 61 cm).
Bequest of the comte
Isaac de Camondo, 1911.

Paul Cézanne (1839–1906).
House of the Hanged Man, 1873.
Oil on canvas,
21⅝ x 26 in. (55 x 66 cm).
Bequest of the comte
Isaac de Camondo, 1911.

Paul Cézanne (1839–1906).
Self-Portrait, c. 1873–76.
Oil on canvas,
25¼ x 20¾ in. (64 x 53 cm).
Gift of Jacques Laroche, 1947.

Paul Cézanne (1839–1906).
The Blue Vase, c. 1885–87.
Oil on canvas,
24 x 19⅝ in. (61 x 50 cm).
Bequest of the comte
Isaac de Camondo, 1911.

ABOVE Paul Cézanne (1839–1906).
The Card Players, c. 1890–95.
Oil on canvas,
18½ x 22⅜ in. (47 x 57 cm).
Bequest of the comte
Isaac de Camondo, 1911.

BELOW Paul Cézanne (1839–1906).
Bathers, c. 1890–92.
Oil on canvas,
23⅝ x 32⅜ in. (60 x 82 cm).
Gift of the baronne
Eva Gebhard-Gourgaud, 1965.

Paul Cézanne (1839–1906).
Woman with a Coffee Pot, c. 1890–95.
Oil on canvas,
51¼ x 37 ¾ in. (130 x 96 cm).
Gift of M. and Mme.
Jean-Victor Pellerin, 1956.

AFTER IMPRESSIONISM

The end of the nineteenth century witnessed a multitude of manifestos, of "isms," of movements destined to split apart, and of innumerable unclassifiable artists, such as Vincent van Gogh, who bore the seeds of Fauvism and of Expressionism.

The period also witnessed a proliferation of exhibition spaces. In Belgium the annual salon of Les Vingt was originated in 1883 by James Ensor, Théo van Rysselberghe, Fernand Khnopff, and Octave Maus. In France in 1884, Odilon Redon, Georges Seurat, and Paul Signac founded the Salon des Indépendants, where the Nabis, the Symbolists, and later the Cubists exhibited. The Salon d'Automne, also in Paris, showed Art Nouveau beginning in 1903, the Fauves in 1905, and major retrospectives of Paul Gauguin in 1906 and Paul Cézanne in 1907. The final Impressionist exhibition, in 1886, marked the emergence of the Neo-Impressionists, with Seurat's *A Sunday on La Grande Jatte.* In his dream of "art-science," the latter explored the theoretical laws of contrast and of optical blending, rendering his paintings in small dots spread out over vast compositions.

In 1891 Gauguin made his first journey to Tahiti; his simultaneously ethnographic and spiritual quest was embodied in paintings that incorporated an eclectic array of quotations from other artists. He had time before his death to transmit his own heritage: Paul Sérusier's *The Talisman* (page 105), fruit of a lesson by Gauguin in Pont-Aven, France, in 1888, became an object of veneration for the Nabis. Despite belonging to the latter group, Pierre Bonnard appears to be an isolated figure at Orsay, as do Gustav Klimt and Edvard Munch. A true "prophet" who went against the grain, Bonnard constantly reinvented himself in the course of his long career.

The symbolic moment of transition to the twentieth century is Henri Matisse's *Luxe, calme et volupté* (page 125). Having joined Signac in Saint-Tropez in 1904, Matisse painted this ultimate Pointillist work, in which space is constructed from broad surfaces of pure color organized according to a newly reinvented perspective. Matisse painted this work in homage to Charles Baudelaire (the title comes from one of his poems) and to Cézanne, thus demonstrating the ambiguity of the nineteenth century as a two-faced Janus looking both forward and back.

Detail of Vincent van Gogh, *The Woman of Arles,* 1888. See page 96.

Georges Seurat (1859–1891).
Model from Behind, 1887.
Oil on wood,
9½ x 5⅞ in. (24 x 15 cm).

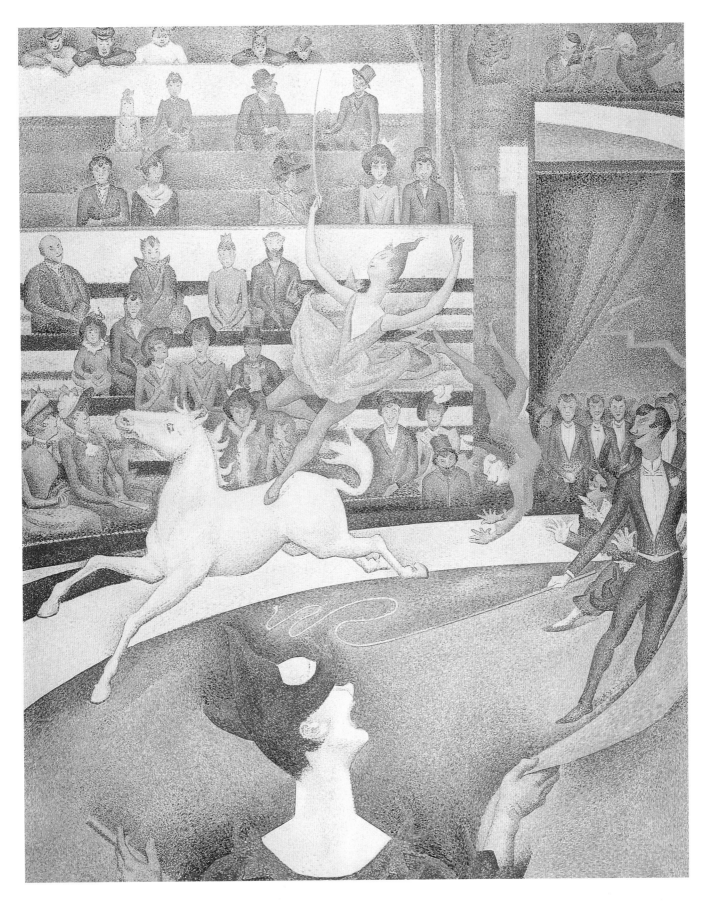

Georges Seurat (1859–1891).
The Circus, 1891.
Oil on canvas,
72¾ x 59¾ in. (185 x 152 cm).
Bequest of John Quinn, 1924.

ABOVE Georges Seurat (1859–1891).
*Port-en-Bessin, Outer Harbour
at High Tide,* 1888.
Oil on canvas,
26 ⅜ x 32⅜ in. (67 x 82 cm).

RIGHT Paul Signac (1863–1935).
Red Buoy, 1895.
Oil on canvas,
31⅞ x 25⅝ in. (81 x 65 cm).
Gift of Dr. Pierre Hébert, 1957.

ABOVE Théo van Rysselberghe
(1862–1926).
The Steersman, 1892.
Oil on canvas,
23⅝ x 31½ in. (60 x 80 cm).
Gift of Mme. Ginette Signac, 1976.

LEFT Henri-Edmond Cross (1856–1910).
The Golden Isles, 1891–92.
Oil on canvas,
23¼ x 21⅜ in. (59 x 54 cm).

Henri-Edmond Cross (1856–1910).
Woman Combing Her Hair, c. 1892.
Oil on canvas,
24 x 18⅛ in. (61 x 46 cm).

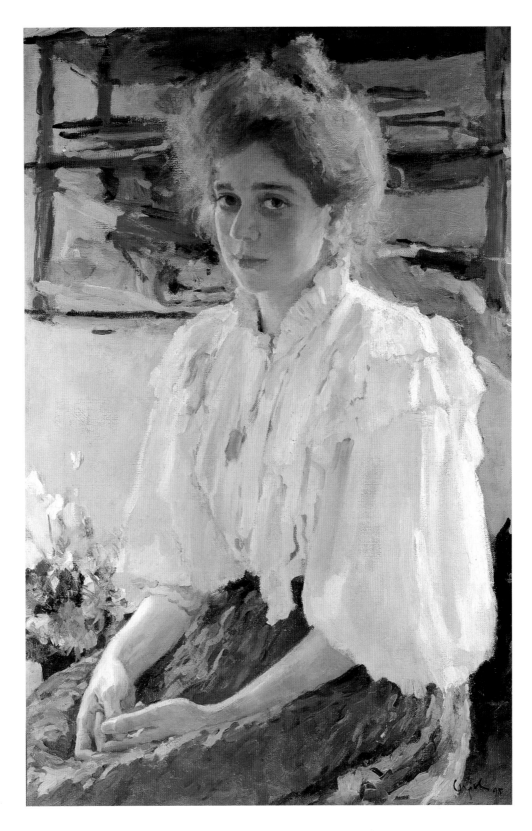

Valentine Alexandrovitch Serov
(1865–1911).
Madame Lvov, 1898.
Oil on canvas,
35⅜ x 23¼ in. (90 x 59 cm).
Gift of Professeur André Lwoff
and M. Stéphane Lwoff, sons of
the model, 1980.

Vincent van Gogh (1853–1890).
The Woman of Arles, 1888.
Oil on canvas,
36¼ x 28⅝ in. (92 x 73 cm).
Gift of Mme. R. de Goldschmidt-
Rothschild, 1952.

Vincent van Gogh (1853–1890).
Self-Portrait, 1889.
Oil on canvas,
25⅝ x 21⅜ in. (65 x 54 cm).
Gift of Paul and Marguerite Gachet,
children of Dr. Paul Gachet, 1949.

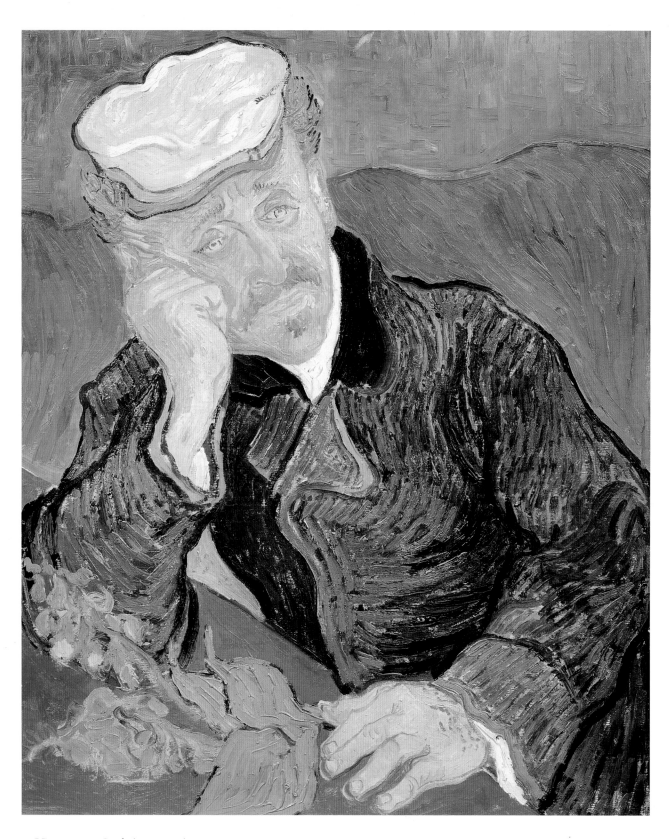

Vincent van Gogh (1853–1890).
Dr. Paul Gachet, June 1890.
Oil on canvas,
26¾ x 22⅜ in. (68 x 57 cm).
Gift of Paul and Marguerite Gachet,
children of Dr. Paul Gachet, 1949.

Vincent van Gogh (1853–1890).
The Church at Auvers, June 1890.
Oil on canvas,
37 x 29⅛ in. (94 x 74 cm).

Paul Gauguin (1848–1903).
The Beautiful Angèle, 1889.
Oil on canvas,
36¼ x 28⅝ in. (92 x 73 cm).
Gift of A. Vollard, 1927.

LEFT Paul Gauguin (1848–1903).
Self-Portrait with Yellow Christ,
1889–90.
Oil on canvas,
15 x 18⅛ in. (38 x 46 cm).

BELOW Paul Gauguin (1848–1903).
Schuffenecker's Studio, or
The Schuffenecker Family,
February–May 1889.
Oil on canvas,
28⅝ x 36¼ in. (73 x 92 cm).

ABOVE Paul Gauguin (1848–1903).
The Meal, or *Bananas,* 1891.
Oil on paper mounted on canvas,
28⅝ x 36¼ in. (73 x 92 cm).
Gift of M. and Mme. André Meyer, 1954.

BELOW Paul Gauguin (1848–1903).
Arearea, 1892.
Oil on canvas,
29¼ x 37 in. (75 x 94 cm).
Bequest of M. and Mme. F. Lung, 1961.

Paul Gauguin (1848–1903).
The White Horse, 1898.
Oil on canvas,
55⅛ x 35¾ in. (140 x 91 cm).

ABOVE Emile Bernard (1868–1941).
Madeleine in the Bois d'Amour, 1888.
Oil on canvas,
54⅜ x 64¼ in. (138 x 163 cm).

BELOW Emile Bernard (1868–1941).
Harvest by the Sea, 1891.
Oil on canvas,
27⅝ x 36¼ in. (70 x 92 cm).

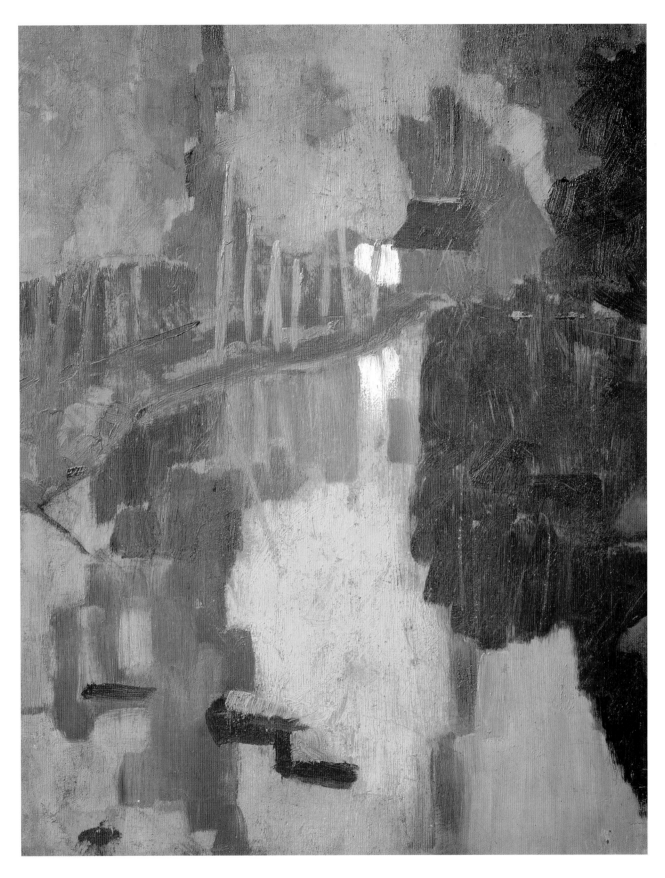

Paul Sérusier (1864–1927).
The Talisman, October 1888.
Oil on wood,
10⅝ x 8⅜ in. (27 x 21 cm).
Acquired through the participation
of Philippe Meyer, 1985.

Henri de Toulouse-Lautrec (1864–1901).
Woman with Black Boa, 1892.
Oil on cardboard,
20⅞ x 16¼ in. (53 x 41 cm).
Gift of the comtesse
Alphonse de Toulouse-Lautrec,
mother of the artist, 1902.

Henri de Toulouse-Lautrec (1864–1901).
The Lady Clown Cha-U-Kao, 1895.
Oil on cardboard,
25¼ x 19⅜ in. (64 x 49 cm).
Bequest of the comte
Isaac de Camondo, 1911.

Henri Rousseau (1844–1910).
War, n.d.
Oil on canvas,
44⅞ x 76¾ in. (114 x 195 cm).

Henri Rousseau (1844–1910).
The Snake Charmer, 1907.
Oil on canvas,
66½ x 74⅜ in. (169 x 189 cm).
Bequest of Jacques Doucet, 1936.

Pierre Bonnard (1867–1947).
The Checked Blouse, 1892.
Oil on canvas,
24 x 13 in. (61 x 33 cm).

ABOVE Pierre Bonnard (1867–1947).
Lazy Nude, 1899.
Oil on canvas,
37 ¾ x 41 ⅝ in. (96 x 106 cm).

BELOW Pierre Bonnard (1867–1947).
The Loge, 1908.
Oil on canvas,
35 ¾ x 47 ¼ in. (91 x 120 cm).

Pierre Bonnard (1867–1947).
Portrait of the Bernheim Brothers, 1920.
Oil on canvas,
65 x 61 in. (165 x 155 cm).
Gift of M. and Mme. Gaston
Bernheim de Villers, 1951.

James Ensor (1860–1949).
Lady in Distress, 1882.
Oil on canvas,
39⅜ x 31⅛ in. (100 x 79 cm).
Gift of Armilde Lheureux, 1932.

August Strindberg (1849–1912).
Wave VII, c. 1900–1901.
Oil on canvas,
22⅜ x 14¼ in. (57 x 36 cm).

Winslow Homer (1836–1910).
Summer Night, 1890.
Oil on canvas,
29⅞ x 40¼ in. (76 x 102 cm).

Maurice Denis (1870–1943).
Sunlight on the Terrace, 1890.
Oil on cardboard,
9½ x 7⅞ in. (24 x 20 cm).

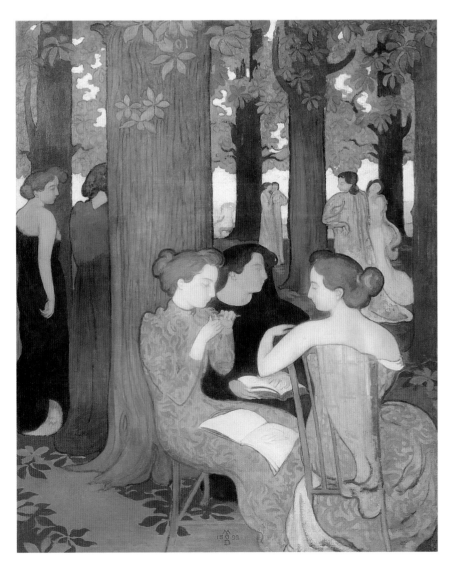

Maurice Denis (1870–1943).
The Muses, 1893.
Oil on canvas,
67½ x 53⅞ in. (171.5 x 137 cm).

Maurice Denis (1870–1943).
Homage to Cézanne, 1900.
Oil on canvas,
70¾ x 94½ in. (180 x 240 cm).
Gift of André Gide, 1928.

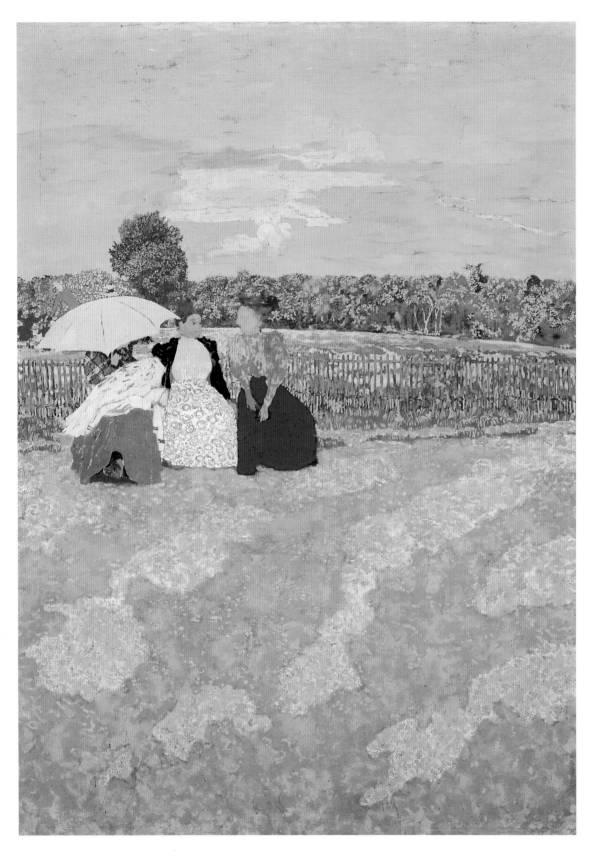

ABOVE Edouard Vuillard (1868–1940).
The Conversation (center panel of
Public Gardens), 1894.
Oil on canvas,
83⅞ x 60⅝ in. (213 x 154 cm).

OPPOSITE Edouard Vuillard (1868–1940).
The Library, 1911.
Oil on canvas,
13 ft. 1½ in. x 9 ft. 9⅝ in. (4 x 3 m).

ABOVE Félix Vallotton (1865–1925).
The Ball, 1899.
Oil on cardboard on wood,
18⅞ x 24 in. (48 x 61 cm).
Bequest of Carle Dreyfus, 1953.

BELOW Félix Vallotton (1865–1925).
Dinner by Lamplight, 1899.
Oil on wood,
22⅜ x 35 in. (57 x 89 cm).

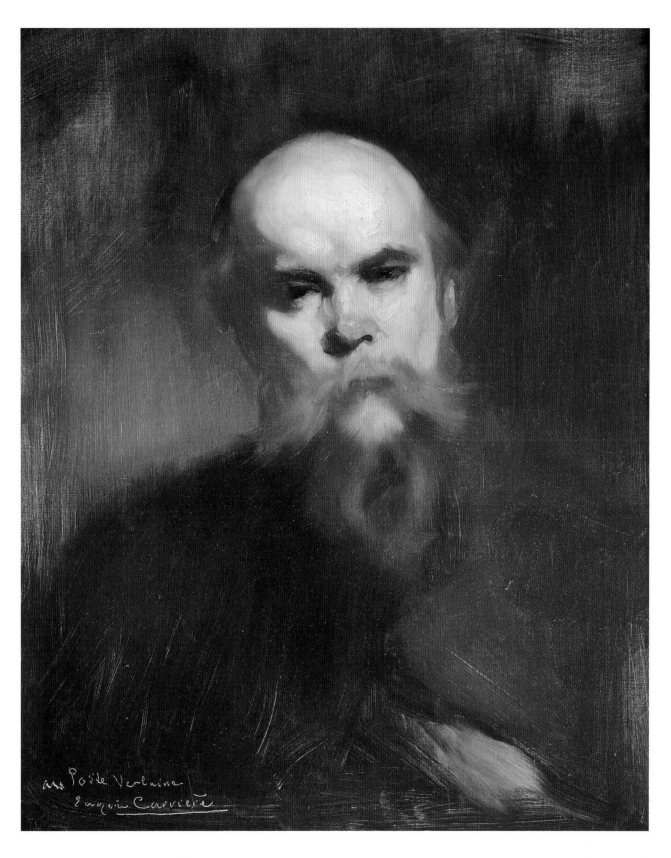

aux Poète Verlaine
Eugène Carrière

Eugène Carrière (1849–1906).
Paul Verlaine, 1891.
Oil on canvas,
24 x 20⅛ in. (61 x 51 cm).

Odilon Redon (1840–1916).
Paul Gauguin, 1903–5.
Oil on canvas,
26 x 21⅜ in. (66 x 54 cm).

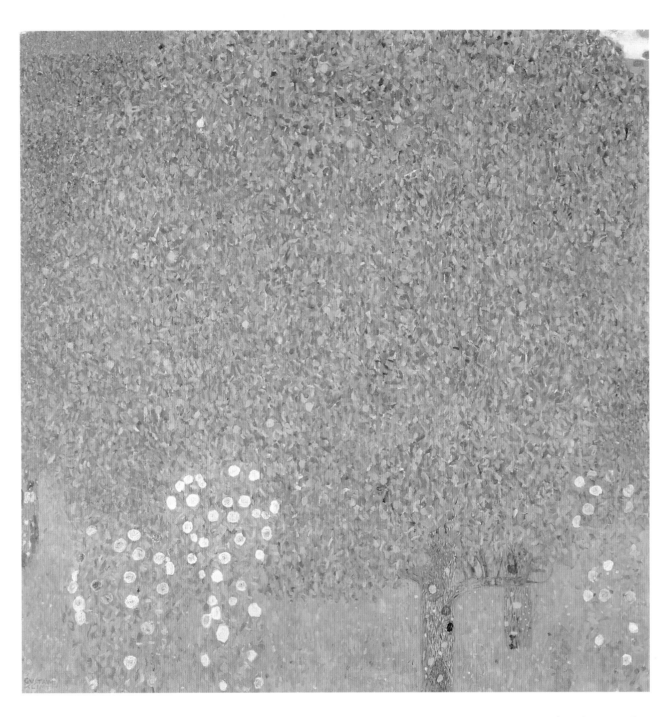

Gustav Klimt (1862–1918).
Roses under the Trees, c. 1905.
Oil on canvas,
43⅜ x 43⅜ in. (110 x 110 cm).

ABOVE Edvard Munch (1863–1944).
Summer Night at Asgarstrand, 1904.
Oil on canvas,
39 x 40⅝ in. (99 x 103 cm).

BELOW André Derain (1880–1954).
Charing Cross Bridge, c. 1906.
Oil on canvas,
31⅞ x 39⅜ in. (81 x 100 cm).
Gift of Max and Rosy Kaganovitch, 1973.

Henri Matisse (1869–1954).
Luxe, calme et volupté, 1904.
Oil on canvas,
38⅝ x 46½ in. (98 x 118 cm).

SCULPTURE

In his review of the 1846 Salon, Charles Baudelaire (who was inspired to write the poem *Le Masque* by Ernest Christophe's sculpture of the same title, page 131) wondered "why sculpture is boring." More costly to produce and often dependent on public commissions, sculpture has been slower to change than painting, even though all the major nineteenth-century movements have been represented in it, from Neoclassicism (Antonio Canova, for example, influenced students at the French Academy in Rome) to Romanticism (despite Théophile Gautier's declaration that "all sculpture is necessarily classical") and Realism (even though Jules Dalou's work lagged behind its pictorial antecedents by twenty years).

Some of the works shown here provoked scandals, including pieces by Auguste Clésinger and Edgar Degas, Auguste Rodin's *Balzac* (page 144), and Jean-Baptiste Carpeaux's *Dance* (page 133). The latter, like Charles Garnier's Opéra for which it was conceived, is a masterpiece of stylistic eclecticism. Such eclecticism imposed itself everywhere, from outdoor monuments to Salon pieces such as Paul Dubois's *Florentine Singer of the Fifteenth Century* (page 134). There was a related tendency to play with diverse materials and techniques; Charles Cordier, like the sculptors of antique Rome, combined bronze and onyx in his *Arab in a Burnoose* (page 131).

Certain painters followed a path blazed by the painter-sculptor-draftsman Honoré Daumier as audacious innovators in sculptural art. Among them were Degas, whose extraordinary *Little Dancer Fourteen Years Old* (opposite and page 140) seems to lack only movement, and Paul Gauguin, who responded to the influence of "primitivism" by returning to direct cutting and polychromy, as in *Be Mysterious,* executed in Brittany in 1890 (page 137).

Synthetism, a style that evolved in the early 1900s, was in part directed against Rodin's genius at modeling and assembling. We see this reaction in the work of Aristide Maillol, whose *Mediterranean* (page 142) prompted André Gide to comment: "It is beautiful, it means nothing, it's a silent work." In work by Emile-Antoine Bourdelle this reaction against Rodin took the form of a new definition of sculpture in relation to architecture. Nonetheless, Rodin remains the great point of intersection between his century and ours. Without fear of narrative or eloquence, he brought together almost all of his sculptural creatures in *The Gates of Hell* (page 145), a state commission for a museum of decorative arts in Paris.

Detail of Edgar Degas, *Little Dancer Fourteen Years Old,* 1881. See page 140.

ABOVE Auguste Préault (1809–1879).
Virgil, 1853.
Bronze medallion,
37⅜ x 33½ x 9⅛ in. (95 x 85 x 23 cm).
Acquired by Napoleon III, 1853.

RIGHT Honoré Daumier (1808–1879).
Portraits of Juste Milieu Celebrities:
Charles Philipon, or
Toothless Laughter, 1831.
Oil-glazed potter's clay,
6⅜ x 5¼ x 3⅞ in. (16 x 13 x 10 cm).

ABOVE François Rude (1784–1855).
Napoleon Awakening to Immortality, 1842.
Plaster model,
84⅝ x 76¾ x 37¾ in. (215 x 195 x 96 cm).

BELOW Auguste Clésinger (1814–1883).
Woman Bitten by a Snake, 1847.
Marble,
22 x 70⅞ x 27⅝ in. (56 x 180 x 70 cm).

Antoine-Louis Barye (1796–1875).
War, 1855.
Model, tinted plaster,
41⅜ x 24⅜ x 35¾ in. (105 x 62 x 91 cm).
Gift of J. Zoubaloff, 1914.

Charles Cordier (1827–1905).
Arab in a Burnoose, 1857.
Bronze and onyx,
16⅞ x 20⅞ x 15¾ in. (43 x 53 x 40 cm).

Ernest Christophe (1827–1892).
The Human Comedy, or
The Mask, 1857–76.
Marble,
96½ x 33½ x 28¾ in. (245 x 85 x 72 cm).

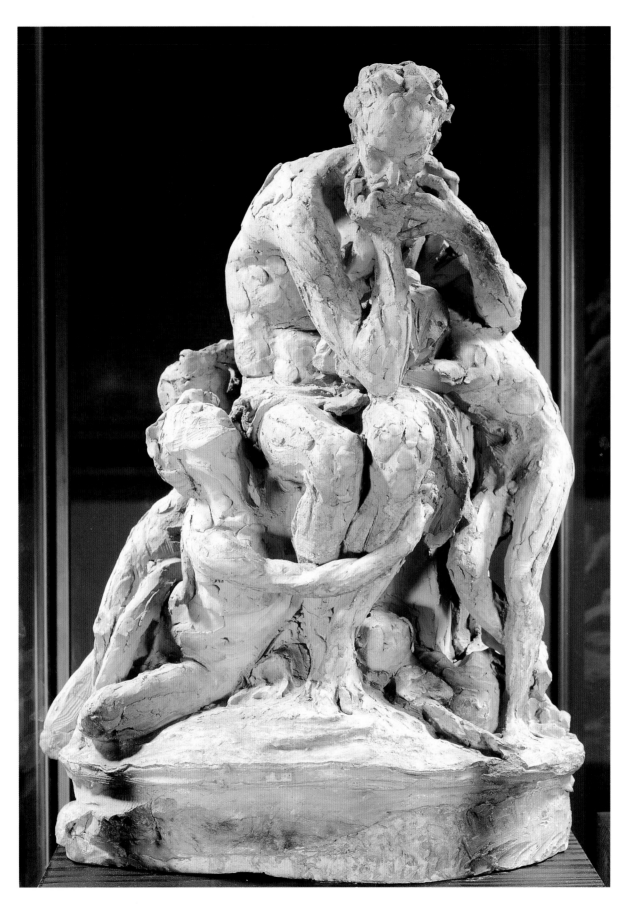

Jean-Baptiste Carpeaux (1827–1875).
Ugolino, 1860.
Terra-cotta sketch,
22⅛ x 16⅛ x 11 in. (56 x 41 x 28 cm).

Jean-Baptiste Carpeaux (1827–1875).
The Dance, 1865–69.
Stone,
13 ft. 8⅜ in. x 9 ft. 9⅝ in. x 4 ft. 8⅜ in.
(4.2 x 2.98 x 1.45 m).

Paul Dubois (1829–1905).
Florentine Singer of the
Fifteenth Century, 1865–67.
Silvered bronze,
61 x 22¾ x 19⅝ in. (155 x 58 x 50 cm).

Emmanuel Fremiet (1824–1910).
Saint Michael, 1879–97.
Hammered copper,
20 ft. 2⅞ in. x 8 ft. 6⅜ in. x 4 ft.
(6.17 x 2.6 x 1.2 m).
Gift of Mme. G. Pasquier.

Louis-Ernest Barrias (1841–1905).
Nature Revealed to Science, 1899.
Polychrome Algerian marbles and onyx,
gray granite, malachite, and lapis lazuli,
78⅝ x 33½ x 21⅝ in. (200 x 85 x 55 cm).

Jean-Léon Gérôme (1824–1904).
Sarah Bernhardt, c. 1895.
Tinted marble,
27¼ x 16⅛ x 11⅜ in. (69 x 41 x 29 cm).
Bequest of the artist, 1904.

ABOVE Paul Gauguin (1848–1903).
Be Mysterious, 1890.
Polychromed limewood bas-relief,
28⅝ x 37⅜ x 2 in. (73 x 95 x 5 cm).

OPPOSITE Georges Lacombe (1868–1916).
Isis, 1895.
Partially polychromed mahogany
bas-relief,
43⅝ x 24⅜ x 3⅞ in. (111 x 62 x 10 cm).

Jules Dalou (1838–1902).
The Peasant, 1899–1902.
Bronze,
77⅝ x 27⅝ x 26¾ in. (197 x 70 x 68 cm).

ABOVE Constantin Meunier (1831–1905).
Industry, 1892–96.
Bronze high relief,
26¾ x 35¾ x 14¼ in. (68 x 91 x 36 cm).

LEFT Camille Claudel (1864–1943).
Maturity, 1893–1903.
Bronze,
44⅞ x 64¼ x 28⅜ in. (114 x 163 x 72 cm).

Edgar Degas (1834–1917).
Little Dancer Fourteen Years Old, 1881.
Patinated bronze, cotton skirt,
and pink satin ribbon,
38⅝ x 13¾ x 9½ in. (98 x 35 x 24 cm).

Pierre-Auguste Renoir (1841–1919).
Madame Renoir, 1916.
Polychromed cement,
32⅜ x 20⅞ x 13⅜ in. (82 x 53 x 34 cm).

Aristide Maillol (1861–1944).
Mediterrannean, or *Thought,* 1905–23.
Marble,
43¼ x 46⅛ x 26¾ in. (110 x 117 x 68 cm).

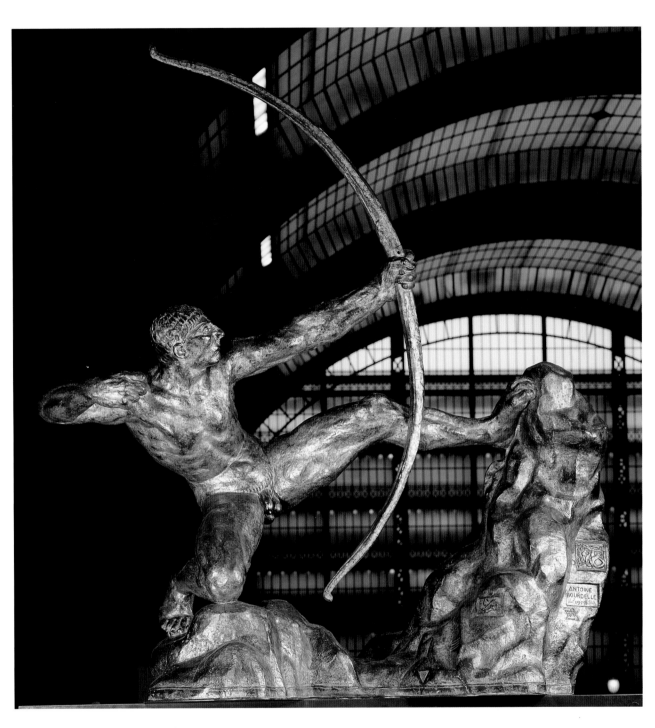

Emile-Antoine Bourdelle (1861–1929).
Hercules the Bowman, 1909.
Gilt bronze,
97⅝ x 97¼ x 43⅜ in. (248 x 247 x 123 cm).

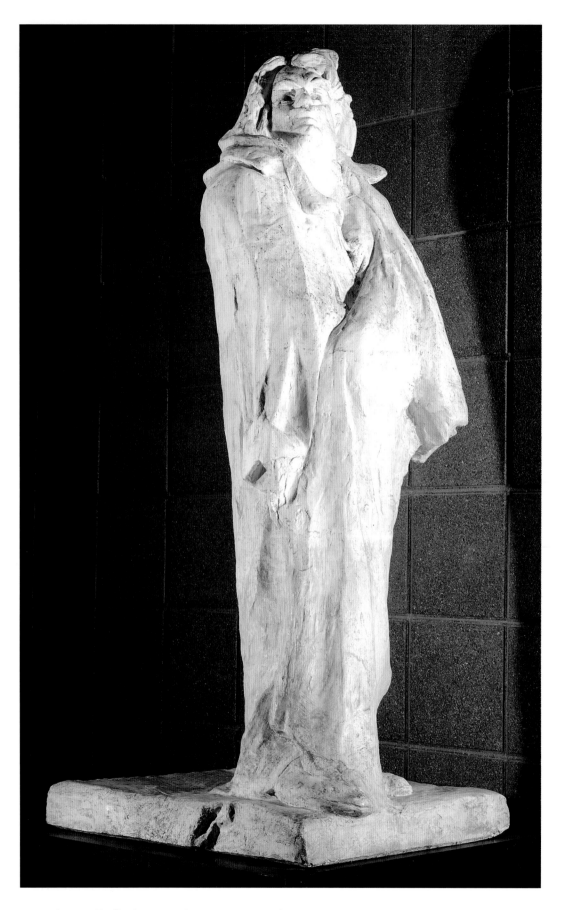

Auguste Rodin (1840–1917).
Balzac, 1898.
Plaster,
108⅜ x 47⅝ x 52 in. (275 x 121 x 132 cm).
Gift of Rodin, 1916.

Auguste Rodin (1840–1917).
Gates of Hell, 1880–1917.
Plaster high relief,
17 ft. x 13 ft. 1½ in. x 3 ft. 1 in.
(5.2 x 4 x .94 m).
Surmounted by *The Shades,*
38⅝ x 35⅜ x 19⅝ in. (98 x 90 x 50 cm).
Gift of Rodin, 1916.

DECORATIVE ARTS

O ur century is formless . . . ," said Alfred de Musset. "We have a little of every century except our own." The term *eclecticism* applies even more to the decorative arts than to painting and sculpture. Even Art Nouveau did not make a total break with eclecticism; for example, the iconography of Emile Gallé's *Hand with Seaweed and Shells* (page 159), his last creation in glass, took its inspiration from various religious sources.

The central idea of eclecticism in the decorative arts is the marriage of art (the beautiful) and industry (the functional). The nineteenth century continued to straddle two sets of ideas, recognizing the necessity of mass production but remaining dependent on artisanal techniques. It continued to dote on the unique piece, on which artists and artisans would collaborate (from Alphonse-Ernest Carrier-Belleuse and Claudius Popelin to Louis Comfort Tiffany and Henri de Toulouse-Lautrec), particularly for the periodic world fairs. The era was marked by two major inventions—mechanical reduction and Jean Christofle's electroplating—but decorative objects remained expensive, and many of them were destined for a newly wealthy clientele that was sometimes lacking in traditions of taste.

Stylistically, eclecticism found sources in everything from ancient Egypt to the eighteenth century. Charles-Jean Avisseau copied Bernard Palissy, while Philippe-Joseph Brocard imitated thirteenth- and fourteenth-century Syro-Egyptian glass. From 1878 to 1889 Japonism paved the way for Art Nouveau.

The idea that structure was inseparable from decoration, that art should aim for a unified totality, shaped the precepts of William Morris and the Arts and Crafts movement in England. Four tendencies can be distinguished in Art Nouveau: abstract and dynamic (Franco-Belgian), organic and vegetal (in Nancy, France), linear and flat (Charles Rennie Mackintosh in Glasgow), and geometric and constructive (in Germany and Austria). The last was associated with the Secession, organized in Vienna in 1897, and with the founding by Josef Hoffmann and Koloman Moser of the Wiener Werkstätte in 1903.

Detail of William Morris, with William De Morgan, *Panel*, c. 1876–77. See page 152.

François-Désiré Froment-Meurice
(1802–1855) with architect Jacques-Félix
Duban and sculptors Jean-Jacques
Feuchère and Geoffroy-Dechaume.
Dressing Table, 1847–51.
Partially gilt silver, gilt and silvered
bronze, engraved iron, and enamel,
height: 86⅝ in. (210 cm).

Charles-Jean Avisseau (1796–1861)
and Octave Guillaume de
Rochebrune (1824–1900).
Goblet and Bowl, 1855.
Polychromed porcelain,
sculpted and inlaid;
goblet: 13¾ x 10¼ in.
(34 x 26 cm);
bowl: 3¼ x 20⅛ in.
(8 x 51 cm).

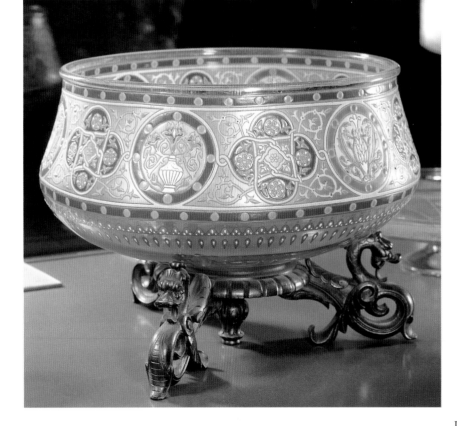

Philippe-Joseph Brocard
(active 1865–1896).
Bowl, 1871.
Blown glass, enameled and gilt,
with original blackened
wood base,
7⅞ x 15⅜ in. (20 x 39 cm).

RIGHT Christofle & Cie, with Mathurin Moreau.
Vase Depicting the Education of Achilles, 1867.
Partially gilt silver,
29½ x 10¼ x 5⅛ in. (75 x 26 x 13 cm).

ABOVE Prosper-Eugène Fontenay
(1823–1887) with Eugène Richet.
Incense Burner, c. 1878.
Gold, translucent enamel, and
enamel paint in relief with diamonds
and lapis lazuli,
8⅜ x 4⅜ in. (21 x 11 cm).

RIGHT François-Désiré Froment-Meurice
(1802–1855) after David d'Angers.
"Patria" Goblet, 1854.
Partially gilt silver, lapis lazuli,
gilt bronze,
7¼ x 4⅜ in. (18.5 x 11 cm).

Charles-Guillaume Diehl
(1811–c. 1885?) with Jean Brandely
and Emmanuel Fremiet.
Medal Cabinet, 1867.
Cedar, ebony, ivory, silver-plated
bronze, and copper,
93⅝ x 59⅜ x 23⅝ in. (238 x 151 x 60 cm).

William Morris (1834–1896)
with William De Morgan.
Panel, c. 1876–77.
66 tiles of polychromed faience,
64¼ x 35⅜ in. (163 x 90 cm).
Gift of the Société des Amis du
Musée d'Orsay, 1989.

François-Rupert Carabin (1862–1932).
Bookcase, 1890.
Walnut and wrought iron,
114¼ x 84⅝ x 32⅝ in. (290 x 215 x 83 cm).

BELOW Otto Eckmann (1865–1902) for
the Königliche Porzellan Manufaktur.
Vase, c. 1897–99.
Porcelain with patinated bronze mount,
20⅛ x 11⅜ x 6⅜ in. (51 x 29 x 16 cm).

ABOVE Christopher Dresser
(1834–1904) for Hukin and Heath,
Birmingham, England.
Soup Tureen, 1880.
Silver plate and ebony,
8⅜ x 12¼ x 9⅛ in. (21 x 31 x 23 cm).

Léopold Van Strydonck (1861–1937).
The Struggle Between Good and Evil, 1897.
Ivory and bronze,
29⅞ x 27⅝ x 13¾ in. (76 x 70 x 35 cm).

Louis Comfort Tiffany (1848–1933) after
Henri de Toulouse-Lautrec (1864–1901).
At the Nouveau Cirque, 1895.
Glass and cabochons,
47¼ x 33½ in. (120 x 85 cm).
Gift of Henry Dauberville in honor
of his children, 1979.

Henry Van de Velde (1863–1957).
Writing Desk, 1898–99.
Oak, gilt bronze, copper, and leather,
50⅜ x 105½ x 48 in. (128 x 268 x 122 cm).

Hector Guimard (1867–1942).
Armchair, 1898–99.
Walnut,
45⅝ x 26¾ x 20½ in. (116 x 68 x 52 cm).

Alexandre-Louis-Marie Charpentier
(1856–1909) with Alexandre Bigot.
Dining Room, c. 1901.
Mahogany, oak, poplar, gilt bronze,
and enameled stoneware,
11 ft. 4 in. x 34 ft. 7 in. x 20 ft. 4 in.
(3.46 x 10.55 x 6.21 m).

LEFT Clément Massier (1845–1917).
Ewer, c. 1893–94.
Faience with metallic luster,
height: 33½ in. (85 cm).
Gift of Mrs. René Bureau.

OPPOSITE Emile Gallé (1846–1904).
Hand with Seaweed and Shells, 1904.
Engraved crystal with additions
and applications,
13 x 5⅛ in. (33 x 13 cm).
Anonymous gift, 1990.

RIGHT René Lalique (1860–1945).
Pendant, 1903–5.
Gold, translucent cloisonné enamel,
brilliants, and aquamarine,
length: 2⅜ in. (6 cm).

Louis Majorelle (1859–1926).
"Orchid" Desk, c. 1903–5.
Mahogany, gilt bronze, and
embossed leather,
37⅜ x 66⅞ x 27⅝ in. (95 x 170 x 70 cm).

Koloman Moser (1868–1918)
for the Wiener Werkstätte.
Music Cupboard, c. 1904.
Oak treated with white lead and
varnished in black, gilded wood, silver-
plated chased metal, white metal, and glass,
78⅜ x 78¾ x 25⅝ in.
(199 x 200 x 65 cm).

Carlo Bugatti (1856–1940).
Chair, c. 1902.
Mahogany, parchment, and
pale wood filleting,
39¼ x 14⅝ x 20⅞ in. (97 x 37 x 53 cm).

ABOVE Josef Hoffmann (1870–1956)
for Jacob & Josef Kohn.
Reclining Armchair, c. 1908.
Laminated, bent, and perforated
beechwood, with mahogany
varnish and latten,
43⅜ x 24⅜ x 32⅜ in.
(110 x 62 x 82 cm).

LEFT Frank Lloyd Wright (1867–1959).
Chair, c. 1904.
Oak and leather,
39¾ x 15 x 18⅝ in. (101 x 38 x 47.3 cm).

PASTELS

Pastels, which had experienced a particular vogue in the course of the eighteenth century, continued in the nineteenth century to be used by artists of every current, from Eugène Delacroix on. A somewhat unpredictable powder, pastel allows for a maximum of experimentation, enabling artists to express the instantaneity of observation as well as visionary allusion.

The works in this chapter range from the audacity of Jean-François Millet's thick crosshatching of pure color to Edouard Manet's increasingly fresh portraits from 1873 on. Edgar Degas appears here as the most consummate draftsman. Though beset by advancing age and increasingly blurred vision, he managed to free himself from all restraints. His technical inventiveness led him to wet his chalk in oil mixtures or to mix pastel and distemper; he practiced stump drawing, left swatches of blank paper, and experimented with monotypes and lithography. In addition to employing these mixed techniques, he piled up multiple layers almost obsessively, exhibiting a taste for variations on a theme, for unprecedented choices in framing his images, for the art of the close-up, as Millet had done. One example of these tendencies is the single plane into which everything is reduced, as if observed "through a keyhole," in *The Tub* (page 167). The boundaries between painting and drawing are abolished.

For the Symbolists, pastel served to communicate the implacable precision of a dream, in which one color often predominates (see *Nocturne at the Royal Park, Brussels,* by William Degouve de Nuncques, page 170), and deliberately esoteric themes (as in Lucien Lévy-Dhurmer's *Medusa,* page 171). The pastels of Odilon Redon, who began using this technique only after passing through an ascetic black period, feature colors of infinite subtlety.

Detail of Mary Cassatt, *Mother and Child Against a Green Background,* or *Maternity,* 1897.
See page 169.

Edouard Manet (1832–1883).
Woman in a Tub, 1878–79.
Pastel on canvas,
21⅜ x 17⅝ in. (54 x 45 cm).
Bequest of the comte
Isaac de Camondo, 1912.

ABOVE Edgar Degas (1834–1917).
The Tub, 1886.
Pastel on cardboard,
23⅝ x 32⅝ in. (60 x 83 cm).

BELOW Edgar Degas (1834–1917).
Two Bathers on the Grass, 1886–90.
Pastel on brown paper,
27⅝ x 27⅝ in. (70 x 70 cm).

Berthe Morisot (1841–1895).
Portrait of Madame Edma Pontillon,
née Edma Morisot, Sister of
the Artist, 1871.
Pastel on paper,
31½ x 25¼ in. (80 x 64 cm).
Bequest of Mme. Pontillon, 1921.

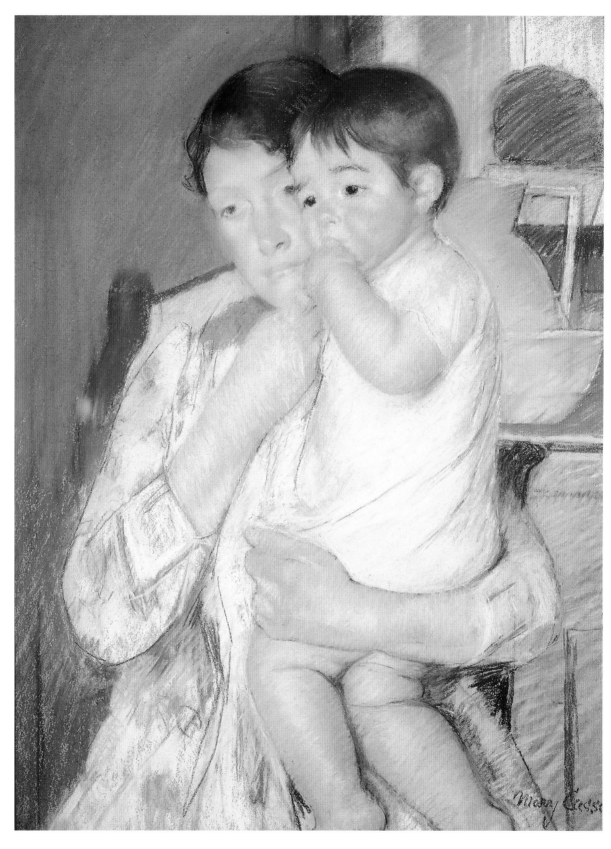

Mary Cassatt (1844–1926).
Mother and Child Against a Green Background, or *Maternity,* 1897.
Pastel on beige paper mounted on canvas,
21⅝ x 18⅛ in. (55 x 46 cm).
Gift of the artist, 1897.

RIGHT William Degouve
de Nuncques (1867–1935).
*Nocturne at the Royal Park,
Brussels,* 1897.
Pastel on paper,
25⅝ x 19⅝ in. (65 x 50 cm).

OPPOSITE Lucien Lévy-Dhurmer
(1865–1953).
Medusa, or *The Angry Wave,* 1897.
Pastel and charcoal on beige
paper mounted on cardboard,
23¼ x 15¾ in. (59 x 40 cm).
Gift of Zagorowsky, 1972.

LEFT Odilon Redon (1840–1916).
Buddha, c. 1906–7.
Pastel on beige paper,
35⅜ x 28⅝ in. (90 x 73 cm).

DRAWINGS AND
WATERCOLORS

For Jean-Auguste-Dominique Ingres, drawing was "the probity of art"; at the other end of the century Pierre Bonnard responded by asserting that "drawing is sensation; color is reasoning."

Nineteenth-century draftsmen loved combining elements, pushing the possibilities of the medium to the extreme. Working on paper, a Jean-François Millet or a Gustave Moreau could be freer than in painting on canvas. The instruments employed might be pen, brush, metalpoint, charcoal, red chalk (Pierre-Auguste Renoir, Aristide Maillol), ink (sometimes as a wash), watercolor (sometimes enhanced with touches of gouache, as in Eugène Boudin and Edouard Manet), pastel, or colored pencils (Henri de Toulouse-Lautrec). In the case of the pencil, the old black chalk was put to rest and, at the time of the Revolution, the Conté pencil was created, which later inspired Camille Corot and Edgar Degas. Later still, a softer pencil was used, which lent itself to a more monumental style in the work of Honoré Daumier and Jean-Baptiste Carpeaux.

Aesthetic elements seem to become liberated in drawing. The cursive line of the caricature predominates in the work of Honoré Daumier or Lautrec; a mixture of writing and drawing characterizes Paul Gauguin's *Noa-Noa* album (page 182), which calls to mind Eugène Delacroix's notebooks from his travels in Morocco. Renouncing color, Georges Seurat preferred a scumble of soft black Conté pencil on rough-grained white paper, which he left showing through; anecdote and reality have disappeared, and all that remains is the allusion to striking, isolated details, as in *The Black Knot* (page 181).

Watercolor, which experienced a revival under English influence, allowed Paul Cézanne to create a prism of transparencies and superimpositions, yielding images that fragment into multiple facets and eliminate linear, finite perspective (page 180). Strangely, the initial pencil outline, which he never followed, is left visible.

Detail of Honoré Daumier, *The Print Collectors*, n.d. See page 174.

ABOVE Gustave Courbet (1819–1877).
*Portrait of Juliette Courbet as
a Sleeping Child,* c. 1841.
Graphite on paper,
7⅞ x 10¼ in. (20 x 26 cm).
Gift of Ernest Courbet, 1916.

BELOW Honoré Daumier (1808–1879).
The Print Collectors, n.d.
Watercolor, gouache, pencil, and
pen and india ink on paper,
10¼ x 12¼ in. (26 x 31 cm).
Bequest of the comte
Isaac de Camondo, 1912.

The Barn Door in the Snow, 1853.
Pencil on paper,
11 x 8⅝ in. (28 x 22 cm).
Bequest of the comte
Isaac de Camondo, 1911.

BELOW Jean-François Millet
(1814–1875).
Fishermen, n.d.
Pencil on paper,
12⅝ x 19⅜ in. (32 x 49 cm).
Bequest of the comte
Isaac de Camondo, 1912.

Léon Bonnat (1833–1922).
Self-Portrait, 1858.
Pen and india ink and wash on paper,
7⅛ x 5½ in. (18 x 14 cm).
Gift of Carle Dreyfus, 1953.

Edgar Degas (1834–1917).
Portrait of Manet, c. 1860.
Graphite and india ink wash
on paper,
13¾ x 7¾ in. (35 x 20 cm).
Gift of Clément Rouart, 1992.

Pierre Puvis de Chavannes (1824–1898).
Study of Four Figures for "Repose," 1863.
Sanguine, pencil, and white gouache
on cream paper,
28⅝ x 16⅞ in. (73 x 43 cm).
Gift of the artist, 1895.

Edouard Manet (1832–1883).
Christ with Angels, 1864.
Graphite, watercolor, gouache, and
pen and india ink on paper,
12⅝ x 10⅝ in. (32 x 27 cm).
Gift of Mme. Emile Zola, 1925.

Gustave Moreau (1826–1898).
The Apparition, 1876.
Watercolor on paper,
41⅝ x 28⅜ in. (106 x 72 cm).
Gift of Charles Hayem, 1898.

ABOVE Paul Cézanne (1839–1906).
The Pots of Flowers, c. 1885.
Graphite and watercolor on beige paper,
9⅛ x 11¾ in. (23 x 30 cm).
Bequest of the comte
Isaac de Camondo, 1911.

LEFT Paul Cézanne (1839–1906).
The Curtains, c. 1885.
Watercolor on paper,
19⅜ x 11¾ in. (49 x 30 cm).
Bequest of the comte
Isaac de Camondo, 1911.

RIGHT Georges Seurat (1859–1891).
The Black Knot, c. 1882.
Conté crayon on paper,
12¼ x 9⅛ in. (31 x 23 cm).

BELOW Vincent van Gogh
(1853–1890).
Père Eloi's Farm, 1890.
Graphite with pen and brown ink
on paper, 18⅞ x 24 in. (48 x 61 cm).
Gift of Paul Gachet, 1954.

LEFT Henri de Toulouse-Lautrec
(1864–1901).
Two Women Waltzing, c. 1894.
Charcoal and oil on tracing paper
mounted on cardboard,
22¾ x 15⅝ in. (58 x 40 cm).
Gift of Claude Roger-Marx, 1974.

RIGHT Paul Gauguin (1848–1903).
Noa Noa Album, folio 75, 1893–97.
Watercolor, pen and black ink, and
woodcut with watercolor on paper,
11¾ x 11 in. (30 x 28 cm).
Gift of Daniel de Monfreid, 1927.

Pierre Bonnard (1867–1947).
Fruit, c. 1930.
Watercolor and gouache with traces of
pencil on paper, 14⅝ x 13 in. (37 x 33 cm).
Gift of Claude Roger-Marx, 1974.

ARCHITECTURE

There have been notable architectural drawings from the Renaissance on, but in the nineteenth century their pedagogical value became particularly valued. In the 1890s a plan was announced to create a "gallery of architectural drawings" at the Louvre. The Musée d'Orsay is in some sense its heir, but with a broader and different sort of ambition than just to create a collection of drawings. What counts more than the individual drawing is the whole of a bequest or a collection, as in the Eiffel bequest, which gathers all the materials that might contribute to a knowledge of the architect.

The Musée d'Orsay also houses picturesque drawings made by architects, travel sketches, finished landscapes, projects for monuments, and presentation drawings prepared with an exhibition or Salon in mind (see, for example, Adolphe Alphand's plan for the never-realized drilling of an artesian well in Passy, France, page 186). Indeed, exceptional creators such as Eugène Viollet-le-Duc attempted all genres, including decorative-art projects and illustrations.

Architectural drawings played a key role in academic competitions and the Prix de Rome; from the Villa Medici, each month the winner of the prize had to send the Institute surveys of antique monuments. Such academic examinations were divided into various types, including "restoration," which allowed for more or less imaginary interpretations, as in Gabriel-Auguste Ancelet's reconstruction of a portico at Pompeii (page 186).

The end of the nineteenth century saw the triumph of the engineer over the traditional architect—a fact symbolized by the functionalist beauty of the Eiffel Tower. Henri Toussaint's rendering of his 1900 project for decorating the tower (page 192) makes it clear that architectural drawing can at times assume the aspect of an ideal, utopian vision, while maintaining the beauty of a technical art.

Detail of André Granet, *Project for the Lighting of the Eiffel Tower for the Exposition Universelle of 1937*, n.d. See page 192.

Gabriel-Auguste Ancelet (1829–1895).
*Reconstruction of a Decoration on the
Portico of Macellum, Pompeii*, 1853.
Pencil, pen and black ink,
india ink wash, watercolor, and
gouache on paper,
18½ x 11 in. (47 x 28 cm).

Adolphe Alphand (1817–1891),
Jean Darcel (1823–?), and
Emile Reiber (1826–1893).
*Project for the Iron Tower for
the Passy Artesian Well*, 1857.
Watercolor with white gouache
highlights on paper,
38⅝ x 23⅝ in. (98 x 60 cm).

ABOVE Max Berthelin (1811–1877).
*The Palace of Industry, Exposition
Universelle of 1855: Transverse Section,*
1854. Pen and black ink with watercolor
on paper, 13 x 26⅝ in. (33 x 67 cm).

BELOW Owen Jones (1809–1874).
*Project for the Interior of a Crystal Palace,
Saint-Cloud, France,* c. 1860–62.
Watercolor, pencil, and colored pencil
on paper, 17⅝ x 47¼ in. (45 x 120 cm).
Gift of the Société des Amis du
Musée d'Orsay.

ABOVE Alphonse-Nicolas
Crépinet (1826–1892).
*Project for the New Paris Opéra:
Perspective View*, 1861.
Graphite and watercolor on paper,
19⅝ x 26¾ in. (50 x 68 cm).

BELOW Alphonse Gosset (1835–1914).
*Rheims Theater: Elevation of the
Principal Facade*, 1867–73.
Pen and black ink, watercolor,
and white gouache highlights on paper,
29½ x 35⅜ in. (75 x 90 cm).

Auguste-Joseph Magne (1816–1885).
*Vaudeville Theater: Elevation of
the Principal Facade,* 1870.
Graphite, gray ink wash, watercolor,
pen and black ink with gouache
and gold on paper,
31⅞ x 19⅝ in. (81 x 50 cm).

Henri-Paul Nénot (1853–1934).
*Project for a Monument to Gambetta
on the Concorde Bridge, Paris,* 1884.
Watercolor on paper,
11 x 27¼ in. (28 x 69 cm).

Louis-Ernest Lheureux (1827–1880).
*Monument to the Glory of the French
Revolution, Bird's-Eye View,* c. 1886–89.
Pencil, pen and black ink, gray wash,
watercolor, and gold on paper,
18⅞ x 33⅞ in. (48 x 86 cm).

Jean-Camille Formigé (1845–1926).
*Palace of Fine Arts on the Champ de
Mars, Exposition Universelle of 1889:
Elevation of Central Entry,* n.d.
Graphite, pen and black ink,
and watercolor on paper,
40¼ x 25⅝ in. (102 x 65 cm).
Gift of the Société des Amis du
Musée d'Orsay.

ABOVE Henri Toussaint (1849–1911).
Project for the Eiffel Tower, Exposition
Universelle of 1900: Elevation, n.d.
Gouache on paper,
35⅜ x 44⅞ in. (90 x 114 cm).
Gift of Mlle. Solange Granet,
Mme. Bernard Granet, and their children.

BELOW André Granet (1881–1974).
Project for the Lighting of the Eiffel Tower
for the Exposition Universelle of 1937, n.d.
Gouache on paper,
32⅜ x 49¼ in. (82 x 125 cm).
Gift of Mlle. Solange Granet,
Mme. Bernard Granet, and their children.

ABOVE Maquette by Rémy Munier
with Eric de Leusse.
Maquette of the Opéra District in 1914.

BELOW Maquette by the Atelier, Rome,
under the direction of Richard Peduzzi.
*The Opéra: Maquette of a Longitudinal
Section, 1982–86.*

PHOTOGRAPHY

"P ersonally," said the photographer Gustave Le Gray, "I am hoping that instead of falling into the domain of industry and commerce, photography will enter into that of art. That is its true and only place." After some debate photography, which had initially been exhibited with scientific and industrial products, was included in the Salon, beginning in 1859.

Photography offered new ideas about the potential of the multiple and about the relationship between art and industry. Skill counted for less than in the other highly formalized arts, and many artists and writers became amateur photographers, including Edgar Degas, Pierre Bonnard, Victor Hugo, and Lewis Carroll. Sometimes even failed attempts can be strangely beautiful, as in Nadar's various portraits of Charles Baudelaire (opposite and page 199). By offering a new vision of reality, photography automatically presented new possibilities, and if there is one notion that is suspect in photography, it is that of objective realism. To give his *Marine* (page 200) its cosmic, timeless quality, Le Gray used two different negatives, one for the sea and one for the sky.

The true invention of photography dates to 1839 and the efforts of Jacques-Louis-Mandé Daguerre, who devised the daguerreotype (a single print on copper—the image is reversed and there is no negative). Next came William Henry Fox Talbot's calotype, founded on the principle of the paper negative. The 1860s saw the industrialization of the medium with extremely rapid technical progress. Painting and photography maintained a two-way dialogue at this time; on the one hand Degas and Marcel Duchamp were benefiting from the research into movement made possible by the chronophotography of Etienne-Jules Marey and Eadweard Muybridge; on the other hand, photographic Pictorialism was promoting a return to aesthetic preoccupations characteristic of painting in the 1850s.

The lyricism of the English school of photography is particularly apparent in the close-up studies by Julia Margaret Cameron (page 199), which in about 1870 foretold the Pictorialists. Among the self-proclaimed Pictorialists, who often specialized in soft-focus imagery, should be mentioned Alfred Stieglitz, Edward Steichen, and Clarence White. And on the margins of Pictorialism are major but unclassifiable artists, such as Eugène Atget, who was later much beloved by the Surrealists.

Detail of Nadar, *Baudelaire Seated on a Louis XIII Chair,* 1855. See page 199.

Louis-Adolphe Humbert de Molard
(1800–1874).
*Louis Dodier (Humbert de Molard's
Butler) as a Prisoner,* 1847.
Daguerreotype,
4½ x 6⅛ in. (11.5 x 15.5 cm).
Gift of the Braunschweig family in
memory of the Galerie Texbraun,
through the intervention of the Société
des Amis du Musée d'Orsay, 1988.

ABOVE William Henry Fox Talbot (1800–1877).
Porcelain Objects on Shelves, from
The Pencil of Nature, 1844.
Talbotype on garnet-colored paper,
5½ x 7⅛ in. (13.9 x 18 cm).
Gift of the Fondation Kodak-Pathé,
Vincennes, 1983.

BELOW Baron Jean-Baptiste-Louis Gros
(1793–1870).
The Parthenon Frieze, Athens, 1850.
Daguerreotype,
4⅜ x 5⅝ in. (11 x 14.5 cm).
Gift of M. Roger Thérond, 1985.

David Octavius Hill (1802–1870) and
Robert Adamson (1821–1848).
The Three Sleepers (Sophie Finlay, Annie
Farney, and the dog Brownie), c. 1845.
Salt print from paper negative,
7⅝ x 7¼ in. (19.5 x 18.2 cm).

Nadar (1820–1910).
*Baudelaire Seated on
a Louis XIII Chair,* 1855.
Unique salt print from destroyed
negative, 8⅜ x 6½ in. (21.2 x 16.4 cm).

Julia Margaret Cameron (1815–1879).
Maud, c. 1867.
Carbon print from glass negative,
12⅝ x 10⅜ in. (32.3 x 26.5 cm).

ABOVE Edouard-Denis Baldus
(1813–1898).
Ruins of the Château de Boves, 1855.
Salt print from paper negative,
13⅜ x 15⅝ in. (34 x 40 cm).

BELOW Gustave Le Gray (1820–1884).
*Marine (Mediterranean Sea—
Mount Agde),* 1856–57.
Albumen print from two glass
negatives, pasted on cardboard,
12¾ x 16½ in. (32.6 x 42 cm).

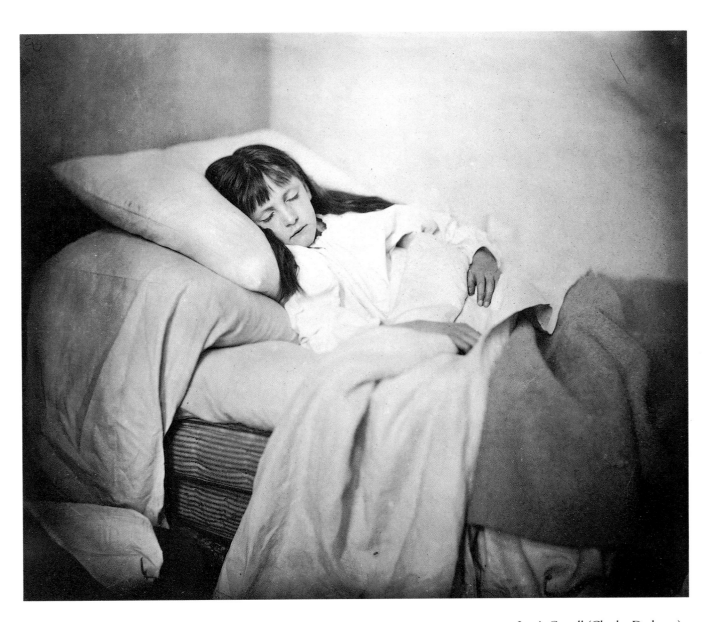

Lewis Carroll (Charles Dodgson)
(1832–1898).
Xie Kitchin Sleeping, 1873.
Albumen print from glass negative,
4⅝ x 5⅝ in. (12 x 14.5 cm).

Paul Burty Haviland (1880–1950).
Landscape in the Snow, n.d.
Carbon print, 2⅝ x 3⅝ in. (7 x 9.5 cm).

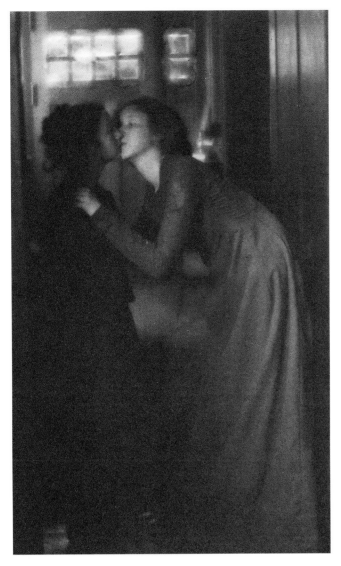

Clarence White (1871–1925).
The Kiss, 1904.
Platinum print,
9⅝ x 5¾ in. (24.7 x 14.8 cm).
Gift of the Société CDF Chimie
Téropolynières, 1985.

Eugène Atget (1857–1927).
Prostitute: Nude in an Interior, 1921(?).
Gelatin silver print,
8⅞ x 6⅞ in. (22.5 x 17.5 cm).
Gift of the Société des Amis du
Musée d'Orsay, 1990.

INDEX OF

ILLUSTRATIONS